# BASEBALL CARDS

Text by
**Larry Schwartz**

PRICE STERN SLOAN
Los Angeles

Published by Price Stern Sloan, Inc.
360 North La Cienega Boulevard, Los Angeles, California 90048

ISBN 0-8431-2469-5

Officially licensed by Major League Baseball

Official Licensee

© 1988 MLBPA
© MSA

**An MBKA Production**

Printed and bound in Hong Kong.

# TEAM LEADERS

## Year-by-Year Batting Leaders

### Home Runs

1962 - Frank Thomas (34)
1963 - Jim Hickman (17)
1964 - Charlie Smith (20)
1965 - Ron Swoboda (19)
1966 - Ed Kranepool (16)
1967 - Tommy Davis (16)
1968 - Ed Charles (15)
1969 - Tommie Agee (26)
1970 - Tommie Agee (24)
1971 - Tommie Agee (14)
         Cleon Jones (14)
         Ed Kranepool (14)

1972 - John Milner (17)
1973 - John Milner (23)
1974 - John Milner (20)
1975 - Dave Kingman (36)
1976 - Dave Kingman (37)
1977 - Steve Henderson (12)
         John Milner (12)
         John Stearns (12)

1978 - Willie Montanez (17)
1979 - Joel Youngblood (16)
1980 - Lee Mazzilli (16)
1981 - Dave Kingman (22)
1982 - Dave Kingman (37)
1983 - George Foster (28)
1984 - Darryl Strawberry (26)
1985 - Gary Carter (32)
1986 - Darryl Strawberry (27)
1987 - Darryl Strawberry (39)
1988 - Darryl Strawberry (39)

### Runs Batted In

Frank Thomas (94)
Frank Thomas (60)
Joe Christopher (76)
Charlie Smith (62)
Ken Boyer (61)
Tommy Davis (73)
Ron Swoboda (59)
Tommie Agee (76)
Donn Clendenon (97)
Cleon Jones (69)


Cleor Jones (52)
Rusty Staub (76)
Rusty Staub (78)
Rusty Staub (105)
Dave Kingman (86)
Steve Henderson (65)



Willie Montanez (96)
Richie Hebner, Lee Mazzilli (79)
Lee Mazzilli (76)
Dave Kingman (59)
Dave Kingman (99)
George Foster (90)
Darry Strawberry (97)
Gary Carter (100)
Gary Carter (105)
Darry Strawberry (104)
Darry Strawberry (101)

### Batting Average

Felix Mantilla (.275)
Ron Hunt (.272)
Ron Hunt (.303)
Ed Kranepool (.253)
Ron Hunt (.288)
Tommy Davis (.302)
Cleon Jones (.297)
Cleon Jones (.340)
Tommie Agee (.286)
Cleon Jones (.319)


Rusty Staub (.293)
Felix Millan (.290)
Cleon Jones (.282)
Del Unser (.294)
Felix Millan (.282)
Lenny Randle (.304)



Lee Mazzilli (.273)
Lee Mazzilli (.303)
Steve Henderson (.290)
Hubie Brooks (.307)
Mookie Wilson (.279)
Mookie Wilson (.276)
Keith Hernandez (.311)
Keith Hernandez (.309)
Keith Hernandez (.310)
Keith Hernandez (.290)
Kevin McReynolds (.288)

## Year-by-Year Pitching Leaders

### Wins

1962 - Roger Craig (10)
1963 - Al Jackson (13)
1964 - Al Jackson (11)
1965 - Jack Fisher, Al Jackson (8)
1966 - Jack Fisher (11)
      Dennis Ribant (11)
      Bob Shaw (11)

1967 - Tom Seaver (16)
1968 - Jerry Koosman (19)
1969 - Tom Seaver (25)
1970 - Tom Seaver (18)
1971 - Tom Seaver (20)
1972 - Tom Seaver (21)
1973 - Tom Seaver (19)
1974 - Jerry Koosman (15)
1975 - Tom Seaver (22)
1976 - Jerry Koosman (21)
1977 - Nino Espinosa (10)
1978 - Nino Espinosa (11)
1979 - Craig Swan (14)
1980 - Mark Bomback (10)
1981 - Neil Allen, Pat Zachry (7)
1982 - Craig Swan (11)
1983 - Jesse Orosco (13)
1984 - Dwight Gooden (17)
1985 - Dwight Gooden (24)
1986 - Bob Ojeda (18)

1987 - Dwight Gooden (15)
1988 - Dave Cone (20)

### Strikeouts

Roger Craig, Al Jackson (118)
Al Jackson (142)
Tracy Stallard (118)
Al Jackson (120)
Jack Fisher (127)



Tom Seaver (170)
Tom Seaver (205)
Tom Seaver (208)
Tom Seaver (283)
Tom Seaver (289)
Tom Seaver (249)
Tom Seaver (251)
Tom Seaver (201)
Tom Seaver (243)
Tom Seaver (235)
Jerry Koosman (192)
Jerry Koosman (160)
Craig Swan (145)
Pete Falcone (109)
Pat Zachry (76)
Pete Falcone (101)
Tom Seaver (135)
Dwight Gooden (276)
Dwight Gooden (268)
Sid Fernandez,
    Dwight Gooden (200)
Ron Darling (167)
Dave Cone (213)

### Earned Run Average

Al Jackson (4.40)
Carlton Willey (3.10)
Galen Cisco (3.61)
Jack Fisher (3.93)
Dennis Ribant (3.21)

Tom Seaver (2.76)
Jerry Koosman (2.08)
Tom Seaver (2.21)
Tom Seaver (2.81)
Tom Seaver (1.76)
Jon Matlack (2.32)
Tom Seaver (2.08)
Jon Matlack (2.41)
Tom Seaver (2.38)
Tom Seaver (2.59)
Nino Espinosa (3.42)
Craig Swan (2.43)
Craig Swan (3.30)
Pat Zachry (3.00)
Mike Scott (3.90)
Craig Swan (3.35)
Tom Seaver (3.55)
Dwight Gooden (2.60)
Dwight Gooden (1.53)
Bob Ojeda (2.57)

Dwight Gooden (3.21)
Dave Cone (2.22)

# 1962

The Mets built from the past (mostly former Dodgers and Giants) under owner Joan Payson and team president George Weiss. The manager was Casey Stengel (fired by the Yankees in 1960). Weiss obtained first baseman Gil Hodges (first Mets homer), second baseman Charlie Neal (first Mets error), third baseman Don Zimmer (started season 0-for-34), catcher Hobie Landrith (first Mets selection in draft) and pitcher Roger Craig (first Mets loss). The Mets played in the oval-shaped Polo Grounds, vacant since the Giants left after the 1957 season. The Mets lost their first nine games before Jay Hook beat the Pirates 9-1. From May 21 to June 6, there was a 17-game losing streak; in July, an 11-game losing streak; and in August, a 13-game losing streak. They finished last in the 10-team league, 60½ games behind the Giants and 24 behind the other expansion team, the Houston Colt .45s. The Mets' record was 40-120. No team in history has ever lost as many games. A look at a few of the pitchers' records: Craig 10-24, Al Jackson 8-20, Hook 8-19, Craig Anderson 3-17 (lost last 16), and Robert L. Miller 1-12 (won final start). Outfielders Frank Thomas (34 homers, 94 RBIs) and Richie Ashburn (.306) were the top players. Marvelous Marv Throneberry was the team symbol. On June 17 it appeared the first baseman had hit a two-run triple, only he was called out for missing first base. When Stengel came out to argue, first-base coach Cookie Lavagetto said, "It won't do any good, Casey. He missed second, too."

RICHIE **ASHBURN**
NEW YORK METS OF

GUS **BELL**
N.Y. METS OUTFIELD

ED **BOUCHEE**
N.Y. METS 1 BASE

CHRIS **CANNIZZARO**
NEW YORK METS C

ELIO **CHACON**

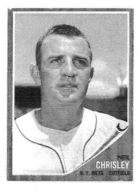

NEIL **CHRISLEY**
N.Y. METS OUTFIELD

ROGER **CRAIG**
N.Y. METS PITCHER

JOHN **DeMERIT**
NEW YORK METS OF

SAMMY
**DRAKE**
N. Y. METS    INF-OF

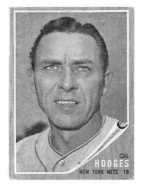

GIL
**HODGES**
NEW YORK METS    1B

JAY
**HOOK**
NEW YORK METS    P

AL
**JACKSON**
N. Y. METS    PITCHER

HOBIE
**LANDRITH**
NEW YORK METS    C

KEN
**MacKENZIE**
N. Y. METS    PITCHER

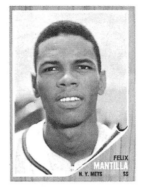

FELIX
**MANTILLA**
N. Y. METS    SS

JIM
**MARSHALL**
N. Y. METS    1 BASE

BOB
**MILLER**
N. Y. METS    PITCHER

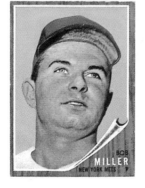

BOB
**MILLER**
NEW YORK METS    P

CHARLEY
**NEAL**
N. Y. METS    2 BASE

CASEY
**STENGEL**
N. Y. METS MANAGER

FRANK
**THOMAS**
NEW YORK METS    OF

# 1963

The Mets lost the opener 7-0 and Casey Stengel said, "We're still a fraud." They improved on 1962, losing only eight games this year before winning their first. Later they had losing streaks of 15 and 11 and a 22-gamer on the road. They were shut out 30 times and hit .219, worst in the majors. They could neither field or pitch, being last in the N.L. in both departments as well. They finished 51-111, in last, 48 games behind the Dodgers. When Jimmy Piersall hit his 100th career homer he ran around the bases back side first. When he was released later with a .194 average, Stengel, whose marvelous sense of humor entertained the fans, said, "There's only room for one clown on this team." Roger Craig (5-22) lost 18 straight, tying a N.L. record. He switched to uniform No. 13 the night he broke the streak, as Jim Hickman hit a grand slam in the ninth to win it for Craig. The Mets received some professional play from rookie second baseman Ron Hunt, the team's top hitter at .272. Al Jackson (13-17) was the only Met with more than nine wins. Marv Throneberry was sent to the minors in May. Hot Rod Kanehl, whose hustle and enthusiasm kept him in the majors for three seasons, led the team in steals with six.

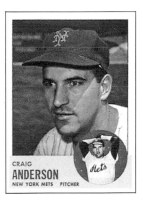

CRAIG
**ANDERSON**
NEW YORK METS   PITCHER

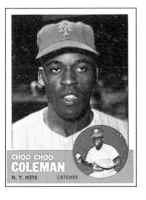

RICHIE
**ASHBURN**
NEW YORK METS   OF

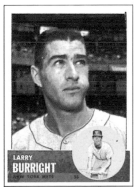

LARRY
**BURRIGHT**
NEW YORK METS   SS

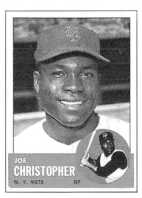

JOE
**CHRISTOPHER**
N. Y. METS   OF

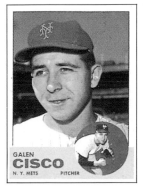

GALEN
**CISCO**
N. Y. METS   PITCHER

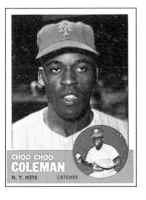

CHOO CHOO
**COLEMAN**
N. Y. METS   CATCHER

CLIFF
**COOK**
NEW YORK METS   3B-OF

ROGER
**CRAIG**
N. Y. METS   PITCHER

PUMPSIE
**GREEN**
NEW YORK METS    SS-2B

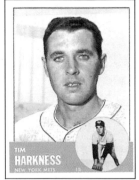

TIM
**HARKNESS**
NEW YORK METS    1B

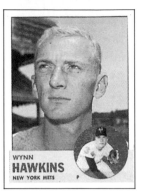

WYNN
**HAWKINS**
NEW YORK METS    P

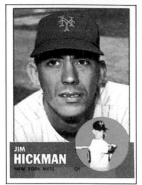

JIM
**HICKMAN**
NEW YORK METS    OF

GIL
**HODGES**
N. Y. METS    1B

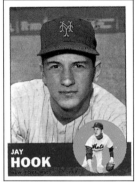

JAY
**HOOK**
NEW YORK METS    PITCHER

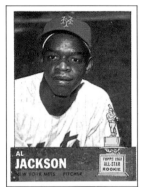

AL
**JACKSON**
NEW YORK METS    PITCHER

TOPPS 1963
ALL-STAR
ROOKIE

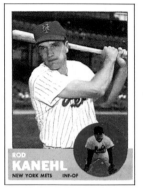

ROD
**KANEHL**
NEW YORK METS    INF-OF

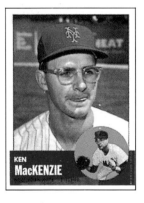

KEN
**MacKENZIE**
NEW YORK METS    PITCHER

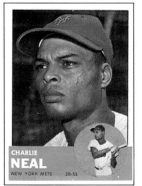

CHARLIE
**NEAL**
NEW YORK METS    3B-SS

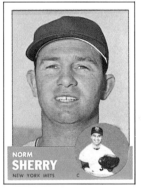

NORM
**SHERRY**
NEW YORK METS    C

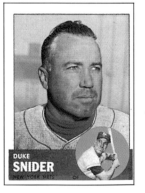

DUKE
**SNIDER**
NEW YORK METS    OF

TRACY
**STALLARD**
NEW YORK METS    PITCHER

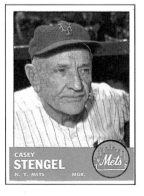

CASEY
**STENGEL**
N. Y. METS    MGR.

SAMMY
**TAYLOR**
N. Y. METS    C

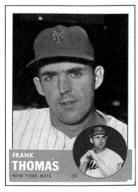

FRANK
**THOMAS**
NEW YORK METS    OF

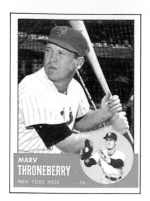

MARV
THRONEBERRY
NEW YORK METS 1b

CARL
WILLEY
NEW YORK METS PITCHER

GENE
WOODLING
NEW YORK METS OF

NEW YORK METS

VETERAN MASTERS
Casey Stengel & Gene Woodling

# 1964

A newspaper in Connecticut received this call from a fan. "I heard the Mets scored 19 runs today." "That's right," the operator said. Then the fan asked, "But did they win?" The Mets still were a laughable team as they finished last again at 53-109, 40 games behind the Cards. They moved into Shea Stadium in Queens, built at a cost of $25.5 million. The attendance was 1,732,597 fans, the second highest in the majors. On Father's Day the fans saw the Phils' Jim Bunning pitch a perfect game against the Amazing Mets. On May 31 a crowd that started at 57,037 saw the Mets lose a doubleheader to the Giants. It lasted nine hours and 52 minutes with the 23-inning second game taking 7:23, a record. The Mets finally had a shortstop who could catch a ball when they obtained Roy McMillan from the Braves. Al Jackson (11-16), Jack Fisher (10-17) and Tracy Stallard (10-20) all lost to every team. Ron Hunt (.303) and rightfielder Joe Christopher (.300, 76 RBIs) were the top hitters.

GEORGE ALTMAN  outfield

LARRY BEARNARTH  p

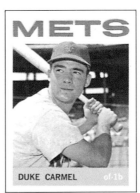

DUKE CARMEL  of-1b

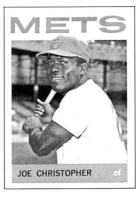

JOE CHRISTOPHER  of

GALEN CISCO  pitcher

CHOO CHOO COLEMAN  c

JACK FISHER  pitcher

JESSE GONDER  catcher

**METS**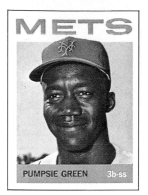

PUMPSIE GREEN 3b-ss

**METS**

TIM HARKNESS 1st base

**METS**

JIM HICKMAN outfield

**METS**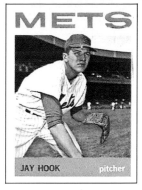

JAY HOOK pitcher

**METS**

RON HUNT 2nd base

**METS**

AL JACKSON pitcher

**METS**

MIKE JOYCE pitcher

**METS**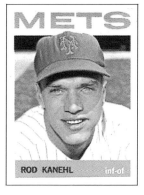

ROD KANEHL inf-of

**METS**

ED KRANEPOOL 1b-of

**METS**

AL MORAN shortstop

**METS**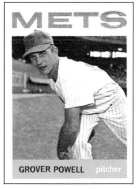

GROVER POWELL pitcher

**METS**

AMADO SAMUEL shortstop

**METS**

CHARLIE SMITH 3b

**METS**

DUKE SNIDER outfield

**METS**

TRACY STALLARD pitcher

**METS**

CASEY STENGEL Manager

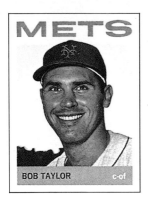

METS

BOB TAYLOR    c-of

METS

FRANK THOMAS    outfield

METS

CARL WILLEY    pitcher

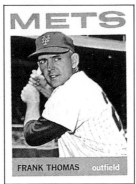

1964 ROOKIE STARS
METS

STEVE DILLON    PITCHER

RON LOCKE    PITCHER

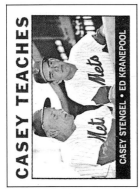

1964 ROOKIE STARS
METS

LARRY ELLIOT    OUTFIELD

JOHN STEPHENSON    CATCHER

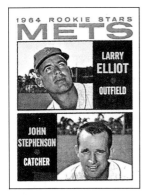

1964 ROOKIE STARS
METS

BILL HAAS    1st BASE

DICK SMITH    1st BASE-OF

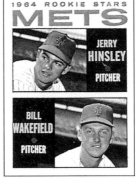

1964 ROOKIE STARS
METS

JERRY HINSLEY    PITCHER

BILL WAKEFIELD    PITCHER

NEW YORK METS

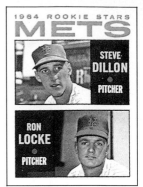

CASEY TEACHES

CASEY STENGEL • ED KRANEPOOL

# 1965

It's hard to believe, but the Mets got worse. They fell to 50-112, last again, 47 games behind the Dodgers. They had the worst batting average (.221) and ERA (4.06) in the league. The Mets were the first N.L. team since 1945 not to have a double-figure winner (Al Jackson 8-20 and Jack Fisher 8-24 were the top winners). Warren Spahn, 44, obtained in the offseason, was released with a 4-12 record. Part of Casey Stengel's "Youth of America," first baseman Ed Kranepool, 20, and rookie rightfielder Ron Swoboda, 21, led the team in batting (.253) and homers (19), respectively. The Reds' Jim Maloney no-hit the Mets for 10 innings then lost in the 11th on a Johnny Lewis homer. Jim Hickman became the first Met to hit three homers in a game. Stengel, 75, ended his managerial career on July 25 when he suffered a fractured hip stepping out of a car. Coach Wes Westrum replaced Stengel as manager. The Mets retired Stengel's No. 37 in September.

PITCHER
LARRY BEARNARTH

CATCHER-COACH
YOGI BERRA

CATCHER
CHRIS CANNIZZARO

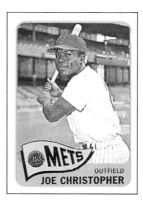

OUTFIELD
JOE CHRISTOPHER

PITCHER
GALEN CISCO

PITCHER
JACK FISHER

CATCHER
JESSE GONDER

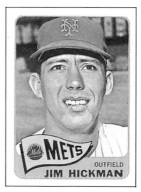

OUTFIELD
JIM HICKMAN

METS

2nd BASE

RON HUNT

METS

PITCHER

AL JACKSON

METS

3rd BASE

BOBBY KLAUS

METS

1st BASE

ED KRANEPOOL

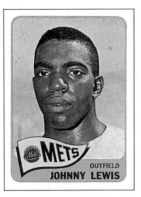

METS

OUTFIELD

JOHNNY LEWIS

METS

PITCHER

RON LOCKE

METS

SHORTSTOP

ROY McMILLAN

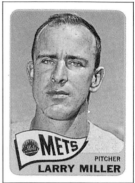

METS

PITCHER

LARRY MILLER

METS

PITCHER

DENNIS RIBANT

METS

3rd BASE-OF

CHARLIE SMITH

METS

P-COACH

WARREN SPAHN

METS

MANAGER

CASEY STENGEL

METS

C-OUTFIELD

HAWK TAYLOR

METS

PITCHER

BILL WAKEFIELD

METS

PITCHER

CARL WILLEY

1965 ROOKIE STARS

TOM PARSONS pitcher

CLEON JONES outfield

METS

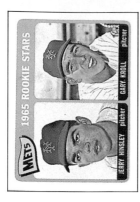

# ≡1966≡

Wes Westrum, in his first full season as manager, led the Mets out of the cellar for the first time in their history. They finished ninth, 28½ games behind the Dodgers with a 66-95 record (13 more wins than their previous high). At the end of July it looked as if the Mets would do even better as they were 47-55, but they finished up 19-40. Third baseman Ken Boyer, obtained from the Cards for Al Jackson and Charlie Smith during the previous November, hit .266 and led the team with 61 RBIs. Ron Hunt, in his final season as a Met, led the team with a .288 average, 13 points higher than rookie leftfielder Cleon Jones' mark. Ed Kranepool, who received an $80,000 bonus after graduating from high school in 1962, led the Mets with 16 homers. Dennis Ribant (11-9, 3.21 ERA) had the first winning season for a Mets starter and was traded after the season to Pittsburgh for outfielder Don Bosch and pitcher Don Cardwell. The Mets drew 1,932,693, more than the N.Y. Giants ever attracted. After the season George Weiss, 72, retired and his assistant, Bing Devine, became team president and GM.

LARRY BEARNARTH    pitcher

ERNIE BOWMAN    infield

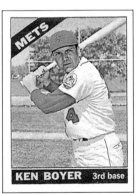
KEN BOYER    3rd base

EDDIE BRESSOUD    infield

CHOO CHOO COLEMAN catcher

JACK FISHER    pitcher

JERRY GROTE    catcher

JACK HAMILTON    pitcher

JIM HICKMAN outfield

CHUCK HILLER 2nd base

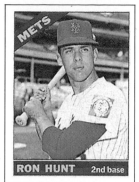
RON HUNT 2nd base

BOBBY KLAUS infield

LOU KLIMCHOCK infield

ED KRANEPOOL 1b

JOHNNY LEWIS outfield

AL LUPLOW outfield

TUG McGRAW pitcher

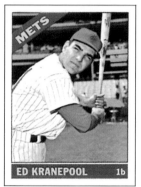
ROY McMILLAN shortstop

DAN NAPOLEON outfield

DENNIS RIBANT pitcher

GORDON RICHARDSON pitcher

JOHNNY STEPHENSON catcher

DICK STUART 1st base

DARRELL SUTHERLAND pitcher

RON SWOBODA outfield

BILL WAKEFIELD pitcher

WES WESTRUM manager

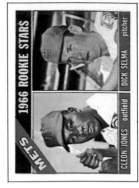

1966 ROOKIE STARS

METS

DICK SELMA pitcher

CLEON JONES outfield

1966 ROOKIE STARS

METS

ROB GARDNER pitcher

DAVE EILERS pitcher

1966 ROOKIE STARS

METS

BILL MURPHY outfield

BILL HEPLER pitcher

METS

10TH PLACE · NATIONAL LEAGUE

# 1967

The Mets used 54 players, including 27 pitchers, and the best by far was rookie righthander Tom Seaver. While at USC, a year earlier, Seaver had been illegally signed by the Braves so the commissioner's office decided on a drawing for any team that would match the Braves' $50,000. The Mets, Phils and Indians said yes and New York won the Seaver lottery. After a year in the minors Seaver joined the Mets and was the N.L.'s Rookie of the Year, going 16-13 with a 2.76 ERA and 18 complete games. "There was an aura of defeatism and I refused to accept it," he said. When Seaver wasn't involved in a decision, the team lost two out of three times. The Mets' record was 61-101, putting them in last place, 40½ games behind the Cards. Outfielder Tommy Davis, obtained from the Dodgers in a deal for Ron Hunt, won the Mets' triple crown (.302, 16 homers, 73 RBIs). Wes Westrum resigned as manager with 11 games left and Bing Devine later left the front office to return home to the St. Louis Cardinals.

SANDY ALOMAR • INF
METS

KEN BOYER 3B
METS

JERRY BUCHEK • 2B-SS
METS

ED BRESSOUD • SS
METS

DON CARDWELL • P
METS

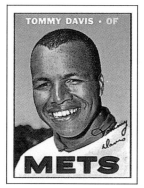

TOMMY DAVIS • OF
METS

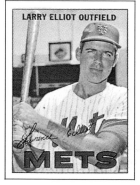

LARRY ELLIOT OUTFIELD
METS

CHUCK ESTRADA • P
METS

JACK FISHER • PITCHER

**METS**

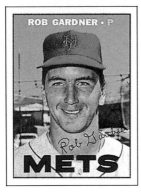

ROB GARDNER • P

**METS**

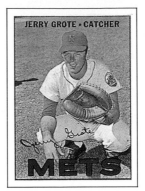

JERRY GROTE • CATCHER

**METS**

JACK HAMILTON PITCHER

**METS**

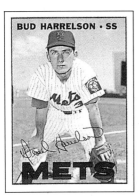

BUD HARRELSON • SS

**METS**

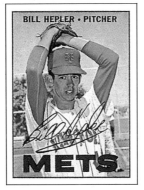

BILL HEPLER • PITCHER

**METS**

CHUCK HILLER • 2B

**METS**

CLEON JONES • OUTFIELD

**METS**

ED KRANEPOOL • 1B

**METS**

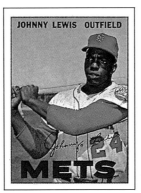

JOHNNY LEWIS OUTFIELD

**METS**

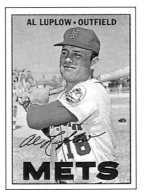

AL LUPLOW • OUTFIELD

**METS**

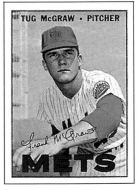

TUG McGRAW • PITCHER

**METS**

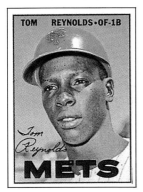

TOM REYNOLDS • OF-1B

**METS**

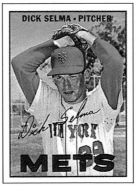

DICK SELMA • PITCHER

**METS**

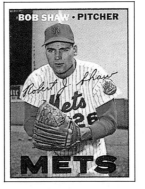

BOB SHAW • PITCHER

**METS**

JOHN STEPHENSON • C

**METS**

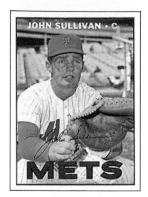

JOHN SULLIVAN • C

**METS**

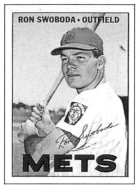

RON SWOBODA • OUTFIELD

**METS**

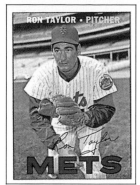

RON TAYLOR • PITCHER

**METS**

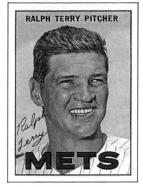

RALPH TERRY PITCHER

**METS**

WES WESTRUM • MGR.

**METS**

METS 1967 ROOKIE STARS

BART SHIRLEY • SS

GREG GOOSSEN • C

METS 1967 ROOKIE STARS

TOM SEAVER • P

BILL DENEHY • P

KRANEPOOL • SWOBODA

**METS MAULERS**

**METS**

# 1968

The Mets got a new manager in Gil Hodges, who had been managing the Washington Senators since 1963. The Mets gave the Senators $100,000 and pitcher Bill Denehy. There also was a new GM with Johnny Murphy replacing Bing Devine. And there was a new centerfielder in Tommie Agee, obtained in a deal with the White Sox for Tommy Davis. Agee, the A.L.'s Rookie of the Year in 1966, didn't fare as well this time around (.217, five homers, 17 RBIs in 132 games). However, another newcomer, Jerry Koosman, did. The rookie lefthander went 19-12 with seven shutouts and a 2.08 ERA to give the Mets a one-two pitching punch. Tom Seaver was 16-12 with a 2.20 ERA. The Mets were fourth in the N.L. in ERA (2.72) and second in shutouts (25). Under Hodges' patient guidance the Mets broke the 70-win barrier for the first time, going 73-89, to finish ninth, 24 games behind the Cards. Hodges, 44, wasn't in the dugout for the finish. He suffered a heart attack in the final week of the season and spent almost a month in the hospital.

TOMMIE AGEE — OUTFIELD METS

DON BOSCH — OUTFIELD METS

JERRY BUCHEK — 2nd BASE METS

DON CARDWELL — PITCHER METS

ED CHARLES — 3rd BASE METS

DAN FRISELLA — PITCHER METS

GREG GOOSSEN — CATCHER METS

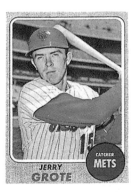

JERRY GROTE — CATCHER METS

BUD
**HARRELSON**
SHORTSTOP
METS

BOB
**HENDLEY**
PITCHER
METS

GIL
**HODGES**
MANAGER
METS

AL
**JACKSON**
PITCHER
METS

CLEON
**JONES**
OUTFIELD
METS

DICK
**KENWORTHY**
3rd BASE
METS

CAL
**KOONCE**
PITCHER
METS

ED
**KRANEPOOL**
1st BASE
METS

PHIL
**LINZ**
INFIELD
METS

J. C.
**MARTIN**
CATCHER
METS

TUG
**McGRAW**
PITCHER
METS

TOM
**SEAVER**
PITCHER
METS

DICK
**SELMA**
PITCHER
METS

ART
**SHAMSKY**
OUTFIELD
METS

DON
**SHAW**
PITCHER
METS

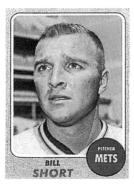

BILL
**SHORT**
PITCHER
METS

RON
SWOBODA
OUTFIELD METS

RON
TAYLOR
PITCHER METS

AL
WEIS
INFIELD METS

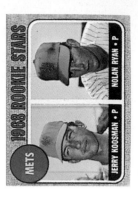

1968 ROOKIE STARS
METS
NOLAN RYAN • P
JERRY KOOSMAN • P

METS
NATIONAL LEAGUE

# 1969

The Mets lost the opener 11-10 to Montreal and some fans undoubtedly thought "same old Mets." But not this year. It was a different team with a new spirit under Gil Hodges. When the season was over the Mets had become the first team to have gone from ninth place to a world championship. Amazing. The Mets were 9½ games back of the Cubs on Aug. 13 before winning 38 of their last 49 to run away with the N.L. East. (Expansion teams in Montreal and San Diego caused the league to form two six-team divisions.) They finished 100-62, eight games ahead of the Cubs. They swept the Braves in three games in the playoffs to win the pennant and then upset the Orioles in five games in the World Series. Amazing. Tommie Agee made two incredible catches to save five runs in the third game of the Series and Ron Swoboda made an unbelievable grab in the fourth game. In the regular season Tom Seaver (25-7, 2.21 ERA) won his last 10 decisions and gained the Cy Young Award. On July 9 he pitched his "imperfect" game as Jimmy Qualls singled with one out in the ninth to become the Cubs' only baserunner. Jerry Koosman went 8-1 from Aug. 17 on to finish 17-9 with a 2.28 ERA. Cleon Jones, removed embarrassingly from leftfield in the middle of a game on July 30 by Hodges, hit a career-high .340.

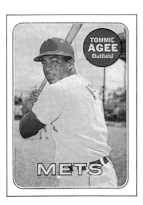

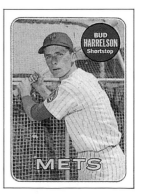

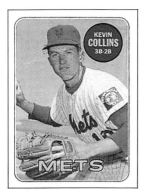

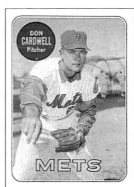

BOB HENDLEY
Pitcher

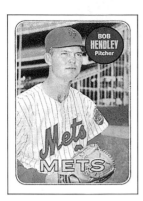

GIL HODGES
Manager

AL JACKSON
Pitcher

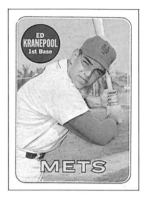

CLEON JONES
Outfield

CAL KOONCE
Pitcher

JERRY KOOSMAN
Pitcher

### The Sporting News

JERRY KOOSMAN
Pitcher
METS

NATIONAL LEAGUE ALL-STARS

ED KRANEPOOL
1st Base

J. C. MARTIN
Catcher

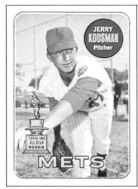

JIM McANDREW
Pitcher

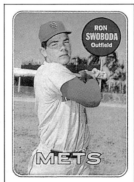

TUG McGRAW
Pitcher

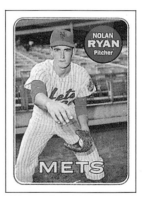

NOLAN RYAN
Pitcher

TOM SEAVER
Pitcher

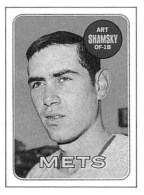

ART SHAMSKY
OF-1B

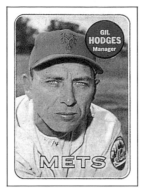

RON SWOBODA
Outfield

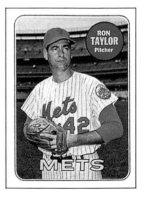

RON TAYLOR
Pitcher

# 1970

The Mets were in contention until they lost six of seven to the Pirates in late September. They finished third at 83-79, six games behind Pittsburgh. Tom Seaver, who struck out a record 10 straight Padres to tie the then-record of 19 in a game, led the N.L. in ERA (2.81) and strikeouts (283). He was 14-5 at the All-Star break but won only four of his last 16 starts to finish 18-12. When healthy, Jerry Koosman was effective (12-7, 3.14 ERA) but injuries limited him to 29 starts. Gary Gentry also had arm problems and dropped from 13-12 as a rookie in 1969 to 9-9. Jim McAndrew (10-14) and Nolan Ryan (7-11) also were disappointing. The biggest bust was new third baseman Joe Foy, acquired from K.C. in the offseason for prize young centerfielder Amos Otis and pitcher Bob Johnson. Otis became a star for the Royals in the 1970s while Foy hit .236 in 99 games for the Mets before being sent to the minors. First baseman Donn Clendenon, a hitting star in the 1969 World Series, had a fine season (.288, 22 homers, 97 RBIs), as did Tommie Agee (.286, 24 homers, 31 steals, Gold Glove).

*Tommie Agee* OUTFIELD

*Ken Boswell* 2ND BASE

*Don Cardwell* PITCHER

*Donn Clendenon* 1ST BASE

*Duffy Dyer* CATCHER

*Joe Foy* 3RD BASE

*Wayne Garrett* 2B-3B

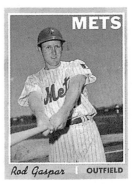
*Rod Gaspar* OUTFIELD

Gary Gentry | PITCHER

Jerry Grote | CATCHER

Bud Harrelson | SHORTSTOP

Gil Hodges | MANAGER

Cleon Jones | OUTFIELD

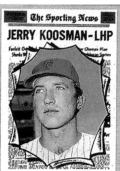

Cal Koonce | PITCHER

The Sporting News
**JERRY KOOSMAN–LHP**

Jerry Koosman | PITCHER

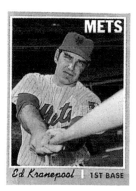

Ed Kranepool | 1ST BASE

J. C. Martin | CATCHER

Jim McAndrew | PITCHER

Tug McGraw | PITCHER

Bobby Pfeil | 3RD BASE

Nolan Ryan | PITCHER

Ray Sadecki | PITCHER

Tom Seaver | PITCHER

Art Shamsky | OUTFIELD

Ron Swoboda | OUTFIELD

Ron Taylor | PITCHER

Al Weis | INFIELD

1970 ROOKIE STARS
METS

MIKE JORGENSEN
1st BASE

JESSE HUDSON
PITCHER

SEAVER WINS OPENER!

N.L. PLAYOFF GAME 1

METS SHOW MUSCLE!

N.L. PLAYOFF GAME 2

RYAN SAVES THE DAY!

N.L. PLAYOFF GAME 3

WORLD CHAMPIONS

The Sporting News
1969 WORLD SERIES • GAME #2

CLENDENON'S HR BREAKS ICE!

The Sporting News
1969 WORLD SERIES • GAME #3

396

AGEE'S CATCH SAVES THE DAY!

The Sporting News
1969 WORLD SERIES • GAME #4

MARTIN'S BUNT ENDS DEADLOCK!

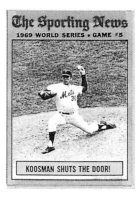

The Sporting News
1969 WORLD SERIES • GAME #5

KOOSMAN SHUTS THE DOOR!

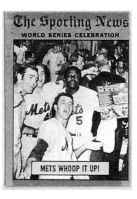

The Sporting News
WORLD SERIES CELEBRATION

METS WHOOP IT UP!

WE'RE NUMBER ONE!

METS CELEBRATE

# 1971

The Mets had the same 83-79 record they had in 1970, but this time it left them 14 games behind the Pirates in a third-place tie with the Cubs. Going into July the Mets were two games out; by the end of it they were 11½ behind after going 9-10. Tom Seaver again led the N.L. in ERA (1.76) and strikeouts (289) and won his 20th game on the final game of the season. He lost 10. Arm and shoulder problems plagued Jerry Koosman (6-11). Nolan Ryan finished 2-10 to go 10-14 and after the season he was traded with three others for Angels infielder Jim Fregosi. The bullpen was strong with left-hander Tug McGraw (11-4, eight saves, 1.70 ERA) and righthander Dan Frisella (8-5, 12 saves, 1.98). Shortstop Bud Harrelson won his only Gold Glove and stole 28 bases. Ed Kranepool hit .280 with a career-high 58 RBIs. Cleon Jones led the Mets with a .319 average and 69 RBIs. The Mets scored a team-record 20 runs in a 20-6 rout of Atlanta.

METS · outfield · tommie agee

METS
bob aspromonte · 3b

METS
ken boswell · 2nd base

METS
dean chance · pitcher

METS
donn clendenon · 1b

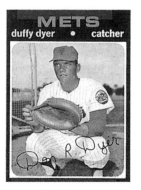

METS
duffy dyer · catcher

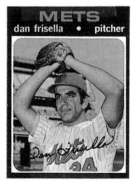

METS
dan frisella · pitcher

METS
wayne garrett · 2b-3b

**METS** — gary gentry • pitcher
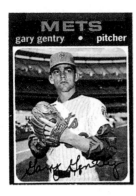

**METS** — jerry grote • catcher
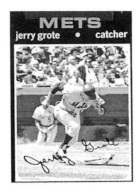

**METS** — bud harrelson • shortstop

**METS** — gil hodges • manager
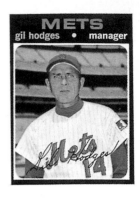

**METS** — cleon jones • outfield
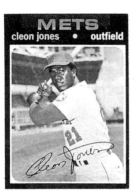

**METS** — mike jorgensen • of-1b

**METS** — jerry koosman • pitcher

**METS** — ed kranepool • 1st base

**METS** — dave marshall • outfield

**METS** — jim mcandrew • pitcher
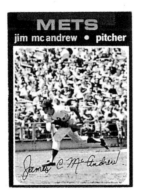

**METS** — tug mcgraw • pitcher

**METS** — jerry robertson • pitcher
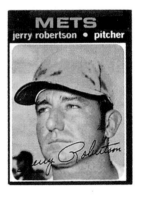

**METS** — nolan ryan • pitcher

**METS** — ray sadecki • pitcher
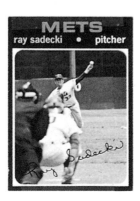

**METS** — tom seaver • pitcher

**METS** — art shamsky • of-1b

ken singleton • outfield

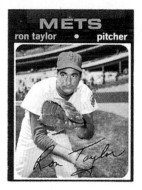

ron taylor • pitcher

al weis • infield

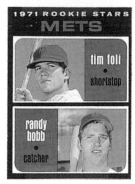

1971 ROOKIE STARS
METS

tim foli • shortstop

randy bobb • catcher

1971 ROOKIE STARS METS

JON MATLACK

TED MARTINEZ

RICH FOLKERS

METS

WORLD CHAMPIONS

# 1972

Tragedy struck on April 2 when manager Gil Hodges died of a heart attack. M. Donald Grant, the Mets' chairman of the board, named coach Yogi Berra to replace him. At the press conference to herald Berra's promotion the Mets also announced they had obtained Montreal rightfielder Rusty Staub for three young prospects—Ken Singleton, Tim Foli and Mike Jorgensen. Staub was hit by a pitch in early June and couldn't grip the bat properly. He played in only 66 games, batting .293. With Staub the Mets broke fast (25-7) and at one time led the division by 6½ games. However, they played eight games below .500 the rest of the way and finished 83-73, in third place, 13½ games behind the Pirates in this strike-shortened season. Jim Fregosi, expected to be the answer to the Mets' ever-present third-base problems, broke his thumb in spring training, then when he came back he hit only .232 with five homers and 32 RBIs in 101 games. Other slumping Mets were Cleon Jones (.245), Tommie Agee (.227) and Bud Harrelson (.215). Tom Seaver (21-12, 2.92 ERA), Rookie of the Year Jon Matlack (15-10, 2.32) and reliever Tug McGraw (8-6, 27 saves, 1.70) had terrific years. The Mets brought Willie Mays back to New York, trading for him in May. Hitting .184 with the Giants, he batted .267 for the Mets.

TOMMIE AGEE

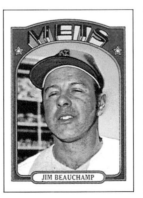

JIM BEAUCHAMP

KEN BOSWELL

KEN BOSWELL IN ACTION

DUFFY DYER

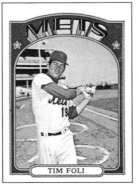

TIM FOLI

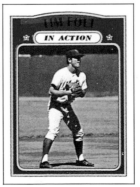

TIM FOLI IN ACTION

BOYHOOD PHOTOS OF THE STARS

JIM FREGOSI

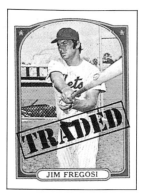

JIM FREGOSI

DANNY FRISELLA

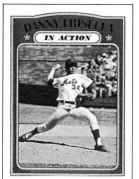

DANNY FRISELLA
IN ACTION

WAYNE GARRETT

GARY GENTRY

JERRY GROTE

DON HAHN

BUD HARRELSON

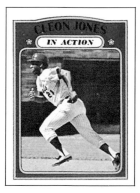

BUD HARRELSON
IN ACTION

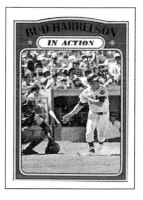

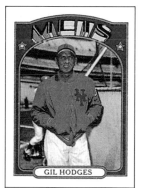

GIL HODGES

CLEON JONES

CLEON JONES
IN ACTION

MIKE JORGENSEN

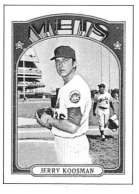

JERRY KOOSMAN

JERRY KOOSMAN
IN ACTION

ED KRANEPOOL

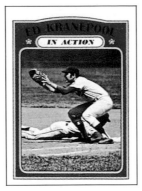

ED KRANEPOOL
IN ACTION

DAVE MARSHALL

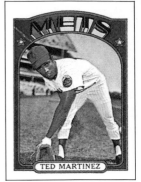

TED MARTINEZ

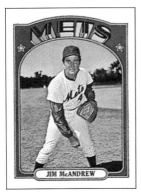

JIM McANDREW

TUG McGRAW

TUG McGRAW
IN ACTION

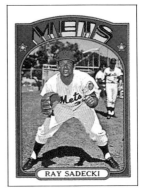

RAY SADECKI

RAY SADECKI
IN ACTION

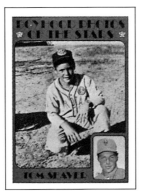

BOYHOOD PHOTOS
OF THE STARS
TOM SEAVER

TOM SEAVER

TOM SEAVER
IN ACTION

KEN SINGLETON

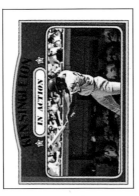

KEN SINGLETON
IN ACTION

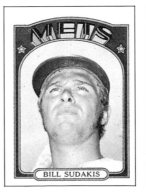

BILL SUDAKIS

CHUCK TAYLOR

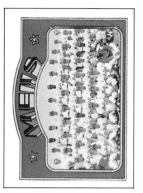

# 1973

"You Gotta Believe!" was the rallying cry of the Mets, Tug McGraw being its creator. And one certainly did on Sept. 20 after a potential game-winning Pirate homer by Dave Augustine in the 13th inning hit the very top of the wall and bounced back to Cleon Jones, who threw a runner out at the plate via a relay man. The Mets won the game, went into first place on the next day and then proceeded to win the pennant. They rallied from last place late in August, going 24-9 in the final five weeks to finish 82-79, 1½ games ahead of the Cards. The .509 winning percentage is the lowest to win any major league title. Then they upset the Reds in the playoffs, three games to two. In the third game, Pete Rose slid hard into Buddy Harrelson trying to break up a DP. Harrelson started swinging and a full-scale brawl developed. The magic ran out after the fifth game of the World Series as the A's took games six and seven to win the championship. Tom Seaver won his second Cy Young Award as he went 19-10 and led the N.L. in ERA (2.08) and strikeouts (251). McGraw came back from a poor start to get 12 saves and five wins in his last 19 appearances. George Stone, acquired before the season with Felix Millan for Gary Gentry and Danny Frisella, went 12-3, helping to make up for Jerry Koosman and Jon Matlack going 28-31. Willie Mays hit .211 and retired after his 22nd season with a .302 average, 660 homers and 1,903 RBIs.

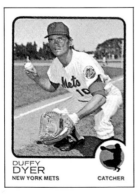

JIM
BEAUCHAMP
NEW YORK METS          OUTFIELD

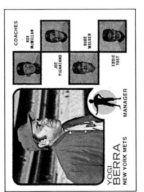

YOGI
BERRA
NEW YORK METS          MANAGER

KEN
BOSWELL
NEW YORK METS          2nd BASE

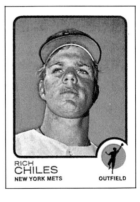

RICH
CHILES
NEW YORK METS          OUTFIELD

DUFFY
DYER
NEW YORK METS          CATCHER

JIM
FREGOSI
NEW YORK METS          3rd BASE

WAYNE
GARRETT
NEW YORK METS          3rd BASE

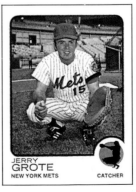

JERRY
GROTE
NEW YORK METS          CATCHER

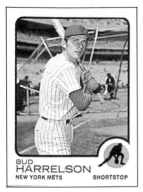

BUD
HARRELSON
NEW YORK METS — SHORTSTOP

PHIL
HENNIGAN
NEW YORK METS — PITCHER

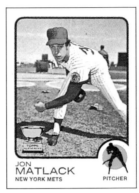

CLEON
JONES
NEW YORK METS — OUTFIELD

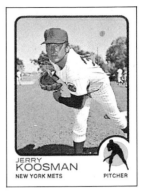

JERRY
KOOSMAN
NEW YORK METS — PITCHER

ED
KRANEPOOL
NEW YORK METS — 1st BASE

TED
MARTINEZ
NEW YORK METS — SHORTSTOP

JON
MATLACK
NEW YORK METS — PITCHER

WILLIE
MAYS
NEW YORK METS — OUTFIELD

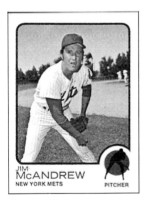

JIM
McANDREW
NEW YORK METS — PITCHER

TUG
McGRAW
NEW YORK METS — PITCHER

FELIX
MILLAN
NEW YORK METS — 2nd BASE

JOHN
MILNER
NEW YORK METS — OUTFIELD

RAY
SADECKI
NEW YORK METS — PITCHER

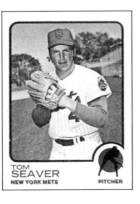

TOM
SEAVER
NEW YORK METS — PITCHER

GEORGE
STONE
NEW YORK METS — PITCHER

BILL
SUDAKIS
NEW YORK METS — CATCHER

NEW YORK METS

# 1974

The Mets had no miracle finish this year as they went 71-91 to fall back into fifth place, 17 games behind the Pirates. Tom Seaver wasn't Tom Terrific (11-11, 3.20 ERA). Tug McGraw was 6-11 with a 4.15 ERA and after the season was traded to the Phils. Jerry Koosman went 15-11 with a 3.36 ERA. While Jon Matlack had a losing record (13-15) he led the N.L. in shutouts with seven and his 2.41 ERA was third best in the majors. First baseman John Milner led the Mets in homers (10) while Rusty Staub led in RBIs (78). Cleon Jones (.282) was the only regular to hit higher than .270. Ed Kranepool was the league's top pinch-hitter at .486 (17-for-35). The Mets lost 4-3 to the Cards in 25 innings. In the final week of the season Bob Scheffing, who had replaced Johnny Murphy as GM in 1970, retired. He was replaced by farm director Joe McDonald.

JIM BEAUCHAMP — METS — NEW YORK — 1B-OF

YOGI BERRA — METS — NEW YORK — MANAGER

KEN BOSWELL — METS — NEW YORK — 2B-3B

DUFFY DYER — METS — NEW YORK — CATCHER

WAYNE GARRETT — METS — NEW YORK — 3rd BASE

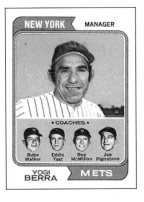

JERRY GROTE — METS — NEW YORK — CATCHER

DON HAHN — METS — NEW YORK — OUTFIELD

BUD HARRELSON — METS — NEW YORK — SHORTSTOP

| NEW YORK CATCHER | NEW YORK OUTFIELD | NEW YORK PITCHER | NEW YORK 1st BASE |
|---|---|---|---|
|  | 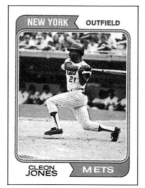 |  |  |
| RON HODGES — METS | CLEON JONES — METS | JERRY KOOSMAN — METS | ED KRANEPOOL — METS |

| NEW YORK SS-2B | | NEW YORK PITCHER | NEW YORK 2nd BASE |
|---|---|---|---|
|  |  |  | 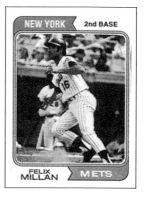 |
| TED MARTINEZ — METS | JON MATLACK P / NEW YORK METS | TUG McGRAW — METS | FELIX MILLAN — METS |

| NEW YORK PITCHER | NEW YORK 1st BASE | NEW YORK PITCHER | NEW YORK PITCHER |
|---|---|---|---|
| 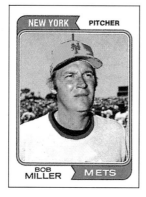 |  |  |  |
| BOB MILLER — METS | JOHN MILNER — METS | HARRY PARKER — METS | RAY SADECKI — METS |

| | NEW YORK OUTFIELD | NEW YORK PITCHER | NEW YORK OUTFIELD |
|---|---|---|---|
|  |  |  |  |
| TOM SEAVER P / NEW YORK METS | RUSTY STAUB — METS | GEORGE STONE — METS | GEORGE THEODORE — METS |

1973
N.L. PLAYOFFS

METS: 3 GAMES • REDS: 2 GAMES

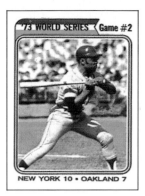

'73 WORLD SERIES    Game #2

NEW YORK 10 • OAKLAND 7

'73 WORLD SERIES    Game #4

NEW YORK 6 • OAKLAND 1

'73 WORLD SERIES    Game #5

NEW YORK 2 • OAKLAND 0

NEW YORK METS

# 1975

Tom Seaver bounced back to win his third Cy Young Award. He went 22-9 to lead the league in victories, winning percentage (.710) and strikeouts (243) while his 2.38 ERA was third best. Seaver became the first pitcher ever to have eight 200-strikeout seasons. His performance, though, wasn't enough to help Yogi Berra keep his job as manager. He was fired on Aug. 6 with the team at 56-53 and was replaced by coach Roy McMillan. The Mets finished 82-80, tied for third with the Cards, 10½ games behind the Pirates. Rusty Staub became the first Met to get 100 RBIs (he got 105) and after the season was involved in a four-player deal in which the Mets acquired Detroit pitcher Mickey Lolich. Dave Kingman was purchased from the Giants in February and while he struck out 153 times and hit .231 he also belted 36 homers with 88 RBIs. Third baseman Joe Torre, obtained from St. Louis, hit only .247. Rightfielder Mike Vail had a 23-game hitting streak, tying the rookie record. After the season, both Casey Stengel and team owner Joan Payson died.

BOB APODACA

GENE CLINES

BOB GALLAGHER

WAYNE GARRETT

JERRY GROTE

DON HAHN

BUD HARRELSON

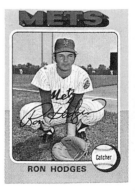
RON HODGES

CLEON JONES

JERRY KOOSMAN

ED KRANEPOOL

TED MARTINEZ

JON MATLACK

TUG McGRAW

FELIX MILLAN

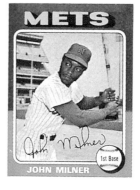

JOHN MILNER

HARRY PARKER

TOM SEAVER

RUSTY STAUB

GEORGE STONE

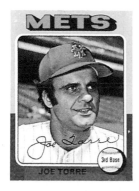

JOE TORRE

# 1976

Joe Frazier, who had won pennants with Mets farm teams the last three years, was the new manager. There was no pennant this year as the Mets finished third at 86-76, 15 games behind the Phils. This was the most Mets wins in any season in the 1970s. Pitching was the key as the Mets' 2.94 ERA led the majors and they were the only team to strike out 1,000 batters (1,025). They had three of the top-10 ERA pitchers in the league in 14-11 Tom Seaver (2.59 ERA, third), 21-10 Jerry Koosman (2.70, fourth) and 17-10 Jon Matlack (2.95, tenth). Seaver led the N.L. in strikeouts again (235). Skip Lockwood was the new ace of the bullpen (10-7, 19 saves, 2.68). Mickey Lolich, though, was a bust (8-13). Dave Kingman was leading the majors with 32 homers on July 19 when he tore ligaments in his thumb diving for a fly ball in leftfield. He was sidelined six weeks. When he returned in late August he hit only five more homers, finishing with 37 in 123 games. He also led the team with 86 RBIs.

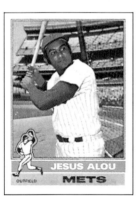

JESUS ALOU — OUTFIELD — METS

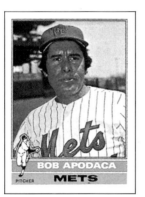

BOB APODACA — PITCHER — METS

RICK BALDWIN — PITCHER — METS

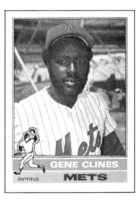

GENE CLINES — OUTFIELD — METS

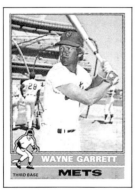

WAYNE GARRETT — THIRD BASE — METS

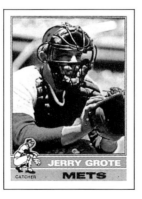

JERRY GROTE — CATCHER — METS

TOM HALL — PITCHER — METS

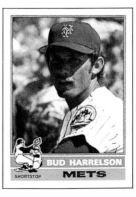

BUD HARRELSON — SHORTSTOP — METS

**DAVE KINGMAN**
FIRST BASE **METS**

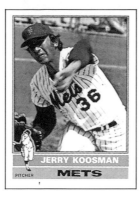

**JERRY KOOSMAN**
PITCHER **METS**

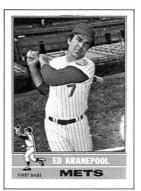

**ED KRANEPOOL**
FIRST BASE **METS**

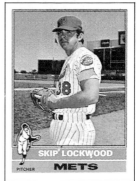

**SKIP LOCKWOOD**
PITCHER **METS**

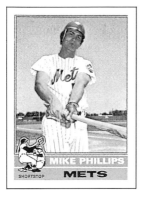

DEC. 12 SPORTS EXTRA 1975
LOLICH COMES TO METS
IN 4-MAN SWAP
PITCHER **MICKEY LOLICH**

**JON MATLACK**
PITCHER **METS**

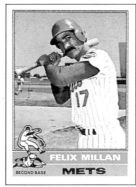

**FELIX MILLAN**
SECOND BASE **METS**

**JOHN MILNER**
OUTFIELD **METS**

**MIKE PHILLIPS**
SHORTSTOP **METS**

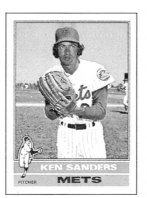

**KEN SANDERS**
PITCHER **METS**

'75 RECORD BREAKER — TOM SEAVER
★ MOST CONSECUTIVE SEASONS
200-OR MORE STRIKEOUTS — 8

**TOM SEAVER**
PITCHER **METS**

**RUSTY STAUB**
OUTFIELD **METS**

**JOHN STEARNS**
CATCHER **METS**

**GEORGE STONE**
PITCHER **METS**

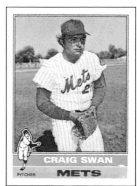

**CRAIG SWAN**
PITCHER **METS**

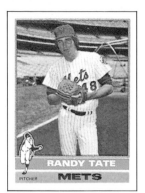

RANDY TATE
PITCHER METS

JOE TORRE
THIRD BASE METS

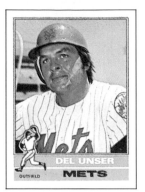

DEL UNSER
OUTFIELD METS

MIKE VAIL
OUTFIELD METS

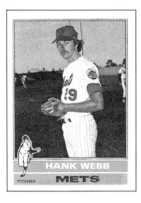

HANK WEBB
PITCHER METS

NEW YORK METS
MGR. JOE FRAZIER

# 1977

It was the year of the Midnight Massacre. On the night of the June 15 trading deadline, Tom Seaver, unhappy about being underpaid at $225,000 a year and with the frugal manner M. Donald Grant ran the franchise, was traded to the Reds for four players. Seaver was 7-3 at the time and went 14-3 with Cincinnati. That same evening the Mets also traded Dave Kingman, who was dissatisfied with the Mets' salary offer and was playing out his option, to San Diego. Earlier in the year Joe Frazier was fired with the team at 15-30, to be replaced by Joe Torre. Without Seaver the Mets finished last for the first time in 10 years as they came in 64-98, 37 games behind the Phils. Jerry Koosman went from 20-game winner to 20-game loser. Jon Matlack had a bad shoulder and bad record (7-15). Nino Espinosa (10-13) was the Mets' only double-figure winner. On the night of July 13 the Mets-Cubs game was victimized by a blackout that paralyzed New York for two days.

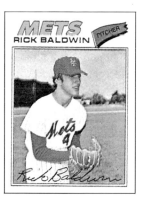

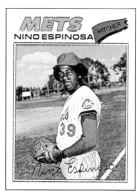

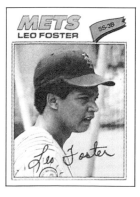

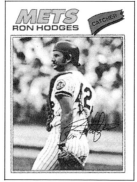

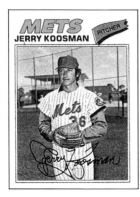
**METS** JERRY KOOSMAN — PITCHER

**METS** ED KRANEPOOL — 1st BASE

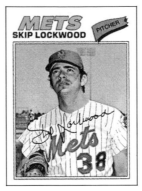
**METS** SKIP LOCKWOOD — PITCHER

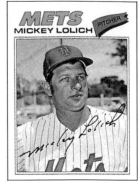
**METS** MICKEY LOLICH — PITCHER

**METS** PEPE MANGUAL — OUTFIELD

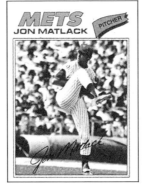
**METS** JON MATLACK — PITCHER

**METS** FELIX MILLAN — 2nd BASE

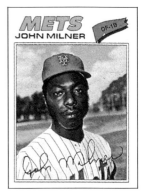
**METS** JOHN MILNER — OF-1B

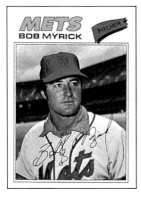
**METS** BOB MYRICK — PITCHER

**METS** MIKE PHILLIPS — SS-2B

**METS** TOM SEAVER — PITCHER

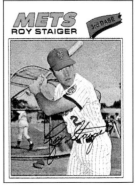
**METS** ROY STAIGER — 3rd BASE

**METS** JOHN STEARNS — CATCHER

**METS** CRAIG SWAN — PITCHER

**METS** JOE TORRE — 1st BASE

**METS** MIKE VAIL — OUTFIELD

# 1978

Pat Zachry, obtained in the Tom Seaver deal, was 10-6 on July 24 when he allowed a hit to Pete Rose during Rose's 44-game hitting streak. When the pitcher returned to the dugout, he kicked the steps and broke his foot. He was out for the year. The Mets also were out for the year. They finished last again, going 66-96, 24 games behind the Phils. Jerry Koosman, in his final Mets season—he was traded to Minnesota in the offseason for Jesse Orosco and Greg Field—had his worst year (3-15). Nino Espinosa was the top winner (11) and loser (15). But the best pitcher was Craig Swan, who went 8-1 in the second half to finish 9-6 and win the ERA title at 2.43. John Stearns hit 15 homers with 73 RBIs and became the first N.L. catcher to steal 25 bases. Centerfielder Lee Mazzilli led the Mets at .273 and hit 16 homers with 61 RBIs. First baseman Willie Montanez, who came to the Mets during the offseason in a complicated four-way deal that sent Jon Matlack to Texas and John Milner to Pittsburgh, led the Mets with 17 homers and 96 RBIs.

BOB APODACA

BRUCE BOISCLAIR

NINO ESPINOSA

LEO FOSTER

BUD HARRELSON

STEVE HENDERSON

RON HODGES

JERRY KOOSMAN

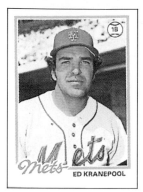
ED KRANEPOOL

SKIP LOCKWOOD

ELLIOTT MADDOX

JON MATLACK

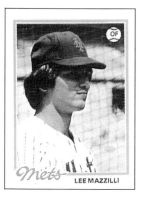
LEE MAZZILLI

FELIX MILLAN

JOHN MILNER

BOB MYRICK

LEN RANDLE

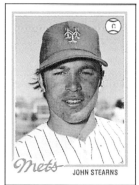
JOHN STEARNS

CRAIG SWAN

JACKSON TODD

AS MANAGER
JOE TORRE
AS PLAYER

MIKE VAIL

BOBBY VALENTINE

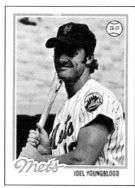
JOEL YOUNGBLOOD

# 1979

The Mets' best moments came in the All-Star Game. That's when Lee Mazzilli tied the game for the N.L. with a home run and sent home the winning run when he walked with the bases loaded. The regular season was another disaster for the Mets (63-99) as they finished last for the third straight season, 35 games behind the Pirates. They went 6-32 at home after the All-Star break. The fans stopped coming to see this losing team as only 788,905 showed up, the lowest the Mets would draw in any full season in their history. Mazzilli led the Mets with a .303 average and his 79 RBIs tied him for the club lead with Rich Hebner, who was acquired from the Phils for Nino Espinosa. Willie Montanez, hitting only .234, was traded back to Texas in August. Rookie Neil Allen (6-10, eight saves) replaced an injured Skip Lockwood (2-5, nine saves) as the bullpen stopper in June. Craig Swan (14-13) was the only pitcher with more than six wins. Ed Kranepool retired after 18 seasons with a .261 average and 118 home runs.

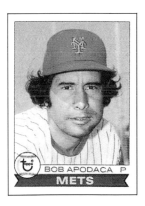

BOB APODACA  P
**METS**

BRUCE BOISCLAIR  OF
**METS**

MIKE BRUHERT  P
**METS**

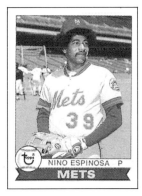

NINO ESPINOSA  P
**METS**

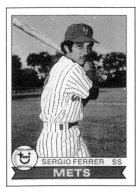

SERGIO FERRER  SS
**METS**

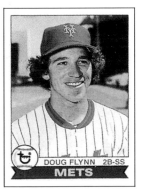

DOUG FLYNN  2B-SS
**METS**

TIM FOLI  SS
**METS**

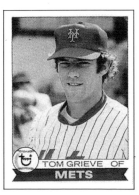

TOM GRIEVE  OF
**METS**

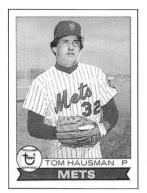

TOM HAUSMAN P
**METS**

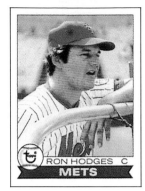

STEVE HENDERSON OF
**METS**

RON HODGES C
**METS**

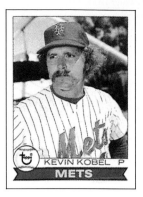

KEVIN KOBEL P
**METS**

JERRY KOOSMAN P
**METS**

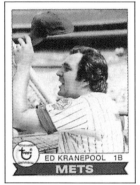

ED KRANEPOOL 1B
**METS**

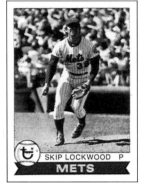

SKIP LOCKWOOD P
**METS**

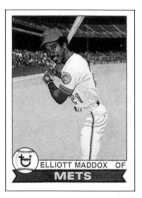

ELLIOTT MADDOX OF
**METS**

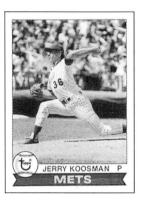

LEE MAZZILLI OF
**METS**

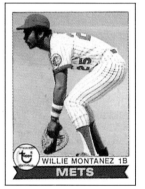

WILLIE MONTANEZ 1B
**METS**

DALE MURRAY P
**METS**

LEN RANDLE 3B
**METS**

**1978 RECORD BREAKER**
JOHN STEARNS
*National League Record: Most Stolen Bases by a Catcher in a Season*

JOHN STEARNS C
**METS**

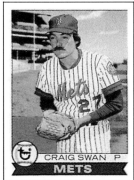

CRAIG SWAN P
**METS**

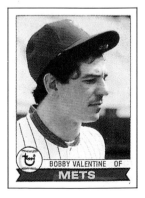

BOBBY VALENTINE OF
**METS**

JOEL YOUNGBLOOD 2B-OF
**METS**

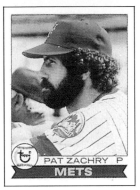

PAT ZACHRY P
**METS**

**METS**

JOE TORRE MANAGER

METS PROSPECTS 1979

JUAN BERENGUER PITCHER
DWIGHT BERNARD PITCHER
DAN NORMAN OUTFIELD

# 1980

In January the Mets were sold by the Payson family for $21.1 million to a group headed by Doubleday & Co. with Nelson Doubleday becoming chairman of the board and Fred Wilpon president. They hired Frank Cashen to replace Joe McDonald as GM. For two-thirds of the season the Mets were an improved team, going 56-57 through Aug. 13 and were only 7 ½ games out of first. But then they went 11-38 to finish 67-95, in fifth place, 24 games behind the Phils. Their 61 homers were the fewest in the majors. Fan favorite Lee Mazzilli led the team with 16 homers and 76 RBIs. The Mets set a club record with 158 steals as Mazzilli got 41, shortstop Frank Taveras had 32 and leftfielder Steve Henderson, obtained in the Tom Seaver deal and the team's leading hitter at .290, stole 23. Rookie Mark Bomback (10-8) was the only pitcher with more than eight victories. Craig Swan, who had signed a five-year, $3.15 million contract, suffered a muscle tear in his shoulder and went 5-9. Neil Allen had 22 saves, tied for fourth in the N.L.

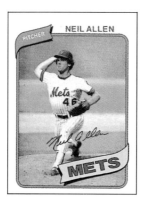

PITCHER NEIL ALLEN

PITCHER BOB APODACA

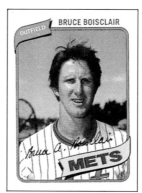

OUTFIELD BRUCE BOISCLAIR

PITCHER RAY BURRIS

OF-1B JOSE CARDENAL

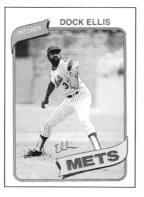

PITCHER DOCK ELLIS

PITCHER PETE FALCONE

SHORTSTOP SERGIO FERRER

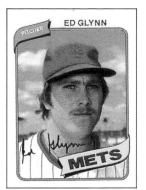
OUTFIELD GIL FLORES
METS

2nd BASE DOUG FLYNN
METS

ED GLYNN
PITCHER
METS

PITCHER ANDY HASSLER
METS

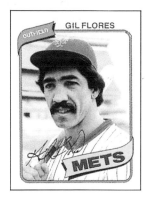
PITCHER TOM HAUSMAN
METS

RICH HEBNER
3rd BASE
Mets
METS

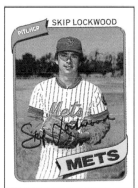
OUTFIELD STEVE HENDERSON
METS

CATCHER RON HODGES
METS

PITCHER KEVIN KOBEL
METS

1st BASE ED KRANEPOOL
METS

PITCHER SKIP LOCKWOOD
METS

OUTFIELD ELLIOTT MADDOX
METS

OUTFIELD LEE MAZZILLI
METS

CATCHER JOHN STEARNS
METS

PITCHER CRAIG SWAN
METS

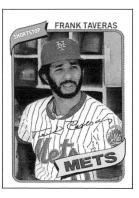
SHORTSTOP FRANK TAVERAS
METS

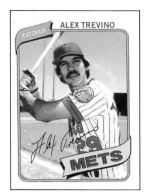

CATCHER ALEX TREVINO

METS

OF-2B JOEL YOUNGBLOOD

METS

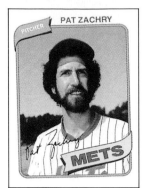

PITCHER PAT ZACHRY

METS

FUTURE STARS

METS

MIKE SCOTT PITCHER

JESSE OROSCO PITCHER

DAN NORMAN OUTFIELD

mgr. JOE TORRE

METS

# 1981

"Same old Mets" as they started out 17-34, which put them in fifth place, 15 games behind the Phils when a 50-day players' strike interrupted the season and caused it to be divided into halves. The Mets did better in the second session, going 24-28 to finish fourth, 5½ games behind the Expos. Joe Torre, who never developed a close relationship with Frank Cashen, was fired as manager on the final day. Cashen traded reliever Jeff Reardon and outfielder Dan Norman for Montreal rightfielder Ellis Valentine in May. Valentine hit .207 with the Mets. Cashen would make better deals in the future. Rookie third baseman Hubie Brooks batted .307, eighth in the N.L. Another rookie, centerfielder, Mookie Wilson, batted .271 and led the team with 24 stolen bases. Dave Kingman, reacquired from the Cubs for Steve Henderson and cash, led the Mets with 22 homers and 59 RBIs though he hit just .221. Neil Allen had 18 saves (third most in the N.L.) and with seven wins tied Pat Zachry for most victories on the Mets. But while Allen lost six games, Zachry tied for the most losses in the majors with 14.

NEIL ALLEN

BILLY ALMON

BOB BAILOR

MARK BOMBACK

HUBIE BROOKS

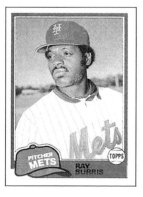
RAY BURRIS

MIKE CUBBAGE

PETE FALCONE

2nd BASE
METS
DOUG
FLYNN

PITCHER
METS
ED
GLYNN

PITCHER
METS
TOM
HAUSMAN

OUTFIELD
METS
STEVE
HENDERSON

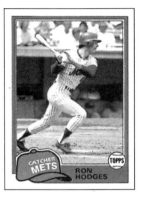

CATCHER
METS
RON
HODGES

PITCHER
METS
ROY LEE
JACKSON

PITCHER
METS
RANDY
JONES

1st BASE
METS
MIKE
JORGENSEN

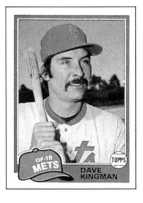

OF-1B
METS
DAVE
KINGMAN

3rd BASE
METS
ELLIOTT
MADDOX

OF-1B
METS
LEE
MAZZILLI

PITCHER
METS
DYAR
MILLER

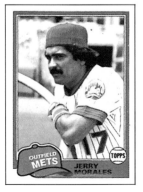

OUTFIELD
METS
JERRY
MORALES

PITCHER
METS
JOHN
PACELLA

PITCHER
METS
JEFF
REARDON

PITCHER
METS
MIKE
SCOTT

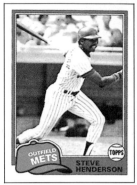

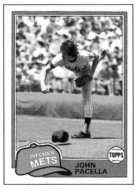
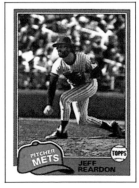
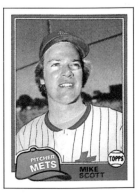

1st BASE METS — RUSTY STAUB

CATCHER METS — JOHN STEARNS

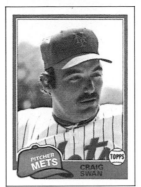

PITCHER METS — CRAIG SWAN

SHORTSTOP METS — FRANK TAVERAS

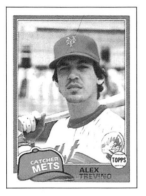

CATCHER METS — ALEX TREVINO

OUTFIELD METS — ELLIS VALENTINE

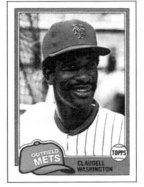

OUTFIELD METS — CLAUDELL WASHINGTON

OF-3B METS — JOEL YOUNGBLOOD

PITCHER METS — PAT ZACHRY

NEW YORK METS — JOE TORRE, MANAGER

METS FUTURE STARS — MOOKIE WILSON OUTFIELD / HUBIE BROOKS 3rd BASE / JUAN BERENGUER PITCHER

# 1982

George Foster, 33 and entering the option year of his contract with the Reds, was traded to the Mets for three mediocre players after agreeing to a five-year contract worth at least $10.2 million. Foster, the last player to hit 50 homers and who three times had 120 RBIs, was no savior. The leftfielder hit .247 with only 13 homers and 70 RBIs. A better deal was made on April 1 when Lee Mazzilli was traded to Texas for minor league pitchers Ron Darling and Walt Terrell. The Mets started off 34-40 under new manager George Bamberger but then they won only 31 of their final 98 games (there was a 15-game losing streak in late August) as they dropped to last at 65-97, 27 games behind the Cards. The team hit .247, next-to-last in the league. Dave Kingman only hit .204, but led the N.L. with 37 homers (tying his club record) and knocking in 99 runs. Mookie Wilson stole a team-record 58 bases. Neil Allen, when not bothered by a colon infection and tendinitis, had 19 saves. Craig Swan, making a comeback from a torn rotator cuff, went 11-7, the only double-figure winner.

**METS**
PITCHER **NEIL ALLEN**

**METS**
SHORTSTOP **BOB BAILOR**

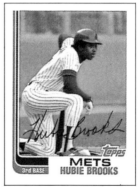

**METS**
3rd BASE **HUBIE BROOKS**

**METS**
3rd BASE **MIKE CUBBAGE**

**METS**
PITCHER **PETE FALCONE**

**METS**
2nd BASE **DOUG FLYNN**

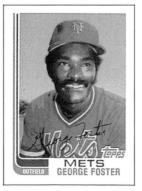

**METS**
OUTFIELD **GEORGE FOSTER**

**METS**
SHORTSTOP **RON GARDENHIRE**

**METS**
PITCHER GREG HARRIS

**METS**
PITCHER TOM HAUSMAN

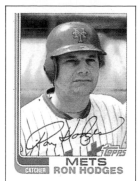

**METS**
CATCHER RON HODGES

**METS**
PITCHER RANDY JONES

**METS**
1st BASE MIKE JORGENSEN

**METS**
OF-1B DAVE KINGMAN

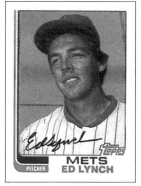

**METS**
PITCHER ED LYNCH

**METS**
OUTFIELD LEE MAZZILLI

**METS**
PITCHER DYAR MILLER

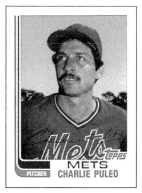

**METS**
PITCHER CHARLIE PULEO

**METS**
PITCHER MIKE SCOTT

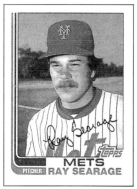

**METS**
PITCHER RAY SEARAGE

**METS**
1st BASE RUSTY STAUB

**METS**
CATCHER JOHN STEARNS

**METS**
PITCHER CRAIG SWAN

**METS**
SHORTSTOP FRANK TAVERAS

**METS**
CATCHER **ALEX TREVINO**

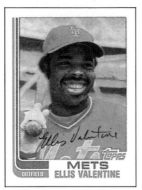

**METS**
OUTFIELD **ELLIS VALENTINE**

**METS**
SHORTSTOP **TOM VERYZER**

**METS**
OUTFIELD **MOOKIE WILSON**

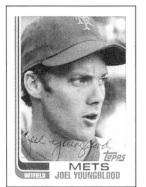

**METS**
OUTFIELD **JOEL YOUNGBLOOD**

**METS**
PITCHER **PAT ZACHRY**

NEW YORK METS
'81 BATTING & PITCHING LDRS.
MIKE SCOTT • 3.90 ERA
HUBIE BROOKS • .307 BA

NEW YORK METS
FUTURE STARS
TIM LEARY Pitcher
TERRY LEACH Pitcher
RON GARDENHIRE Shortstop

# 1983

After five and a half seasons in Cincinnati, Tom Seaver came home to New York. Frank Cashen obtained him for pitcher Charlie Puleo and two minor leaguers in the offseason. Seaver pitched decently (3.55 ERA) but had little support from his teammates (the Mets were last in the N.L. in runs) and went 9-14. The Mets finished last at 68-94, 22 games behind the Phils. However, there was reason for optimism. Rightfielder Darryl Strawberry, brought up in early May, was the N.L.'s Rookie of the Year (.257, 26 homers, 74 RBIs, 19 steals). Lefthander Jesse Orosco emerged as one of the game's top relievers (13-7, 17 saves, 1.47 ERA) and righthander Doug Sisk complemented him well (11 saves, 2.24 ERA). Keith Hernandez, a solid hitter and the best-fielding first baseman in baseball, was obtained from the Cards on June 15 for pitchers Neil Allen and Rick Ownbey. Hernandez hit .306 for the Mets. His presence relegated stone-fingered Dave Kingman to the bench. The moody slugger was released at the end of the season. George Foster flashed power again, leading the club with 28 homers and 90 RBIs, but batted just .241. George Bamberger quit as manager in early June with the Mets at 16-30. Coach Frank Howard replaced him for the rest of the season.

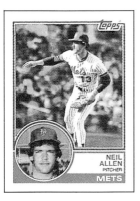
NEIL ALLEN
PITCHER
METS

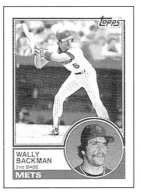
WALLY BACKMAN
2nd BASE
METS

BOB BAILOR
3B-SHORTSTOP-2B
METS

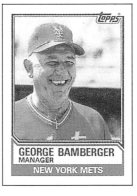
GEORGE BAMBERGER
MANAGER
NEW YORK METS

HUBIE BROOKS
3rd BASE
METS

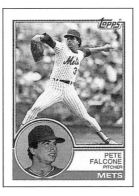
PETE FALCONE
PITCHER
METS

GEORGE FOSTER
OUTFIELD
METS

RON GARDENHIRE
SHORTSTOP
METS

BRIAN
GILES
2nd BASE-SS
**METS**

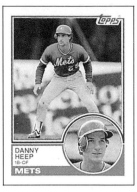

DANNY
HEEP
1B-OF
**METS**

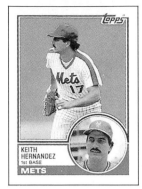

KEITH
HERNANDEZ
1st BASE
**METS**

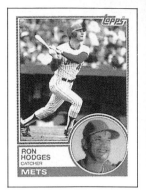

RON
HODGES
CATCHER
**METS**

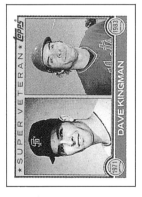

FRANK HOWARD
MANAGER
**NEW YORK METS**

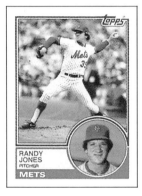

RANDY
JONES
PITCHER
**METS**

MIKE
JORGENSEN
OUTFIELD-1st BASE
**METS**

DAVE
KINGMAN
1st BASE
**METS**

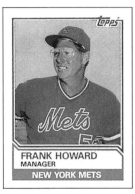

★ SUPER VETERAN ★ Topps
1983
1971
DAVE KINGMAN

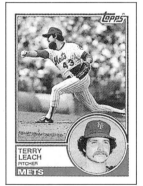

TERRY
LEACH
PITCHER
**METS**

ED
LYNCH
PITCHER
**METS**

JESSE
OROSCO
PITCHER
**METS**

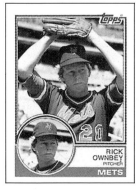

RICK
OWNBEY
PITCHER
**METS**

CHARLIE
PULEO
PITCHER
**METS**

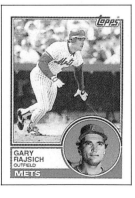

GARY
RAJSICH
OUTFIELD
**METS**

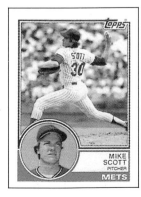

MIKE
SCOTT
PITCHER
**METS**

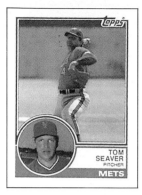

TOM
SEAVER
PITCHER
**METS**

DOUG
SISK
PITCHER
**METS**

RUSTY
STAUB
1st BASE-OUTFIELD
**METS**

★ SUPER VETERAN ★  RUSTY STAUB

JOHN
STEARNS
CATCHER
**METS**

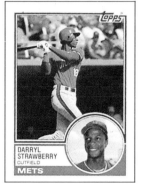

DARRYL
STRAWBERRY
OUTFIELD
**METS**

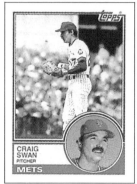

CRAIG
SWAN
PITCHER
**METS**

MIKE
TORREZ
PITCHER
**METS**

ELLIS
VALENTINE
OUTFIELD
**METS**

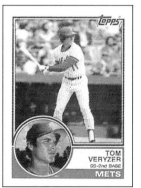

TOM
VERYZER
SS-2nd BASE
**METS**

MOOKIE
WILSON
OUTFIELD
**METS**

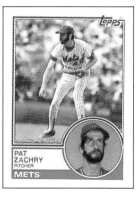

PAT
ZACHRY
PITCHER
**METS**

1982 BATTING & PITCHING LEADERS

CRAIG SWAN
3.35 ERA

MOOKIE WILSON
279 BA

NEW YORK METS

# 1984

The Mets lost their first franchise pitcher and gained a new one. Tom Seaver was selected by the White Sox under the free-agent compensation rules. Dwight Gooden, 19, became the Mets' new hero. Dr. K led the majors with 276 strikeouts, breaking Herb Scores's rookie mark of 245, averaging a record 11.39 strikeouts per nine innings. He went 17-9 with a 2.60 ERA (second in the N.L.), was the youngest player in All-Star history and was voted Rookie of the Year. His pitching helped the Mets become contenders as they finished second under new manager Davey Johnson at 90-72, 6½ games behind the Cubs. On July 27 the Mets led Chicago by 4½ games but they lost seven straight to them in a 13-day span and fell 4½ back. Another rookie, Ron Darling, also was a sweetheart of a pitcher (12-9, 3.81 ERA). Darryl Strawberry, despite not hitting any homers in May and August, finished with 26 homers (fourth in the league) and 97 RBIs. Keith Hernandez hit .311 (seventh in the N.L.), had an on-base percentage of .409 and drove in 94 runs. Hubie Brooks, moved from third base to shortstop late in the season to fill a big need, hit .283 with 16 homers and 73 RBIs. The bullpen was superb again with Jesse Orosco (10-6, team-record 31 saves, 2.59 ERA) and Doug Sisk (15 saves, 2.09).

TUCKER ASHFORD 3B

BOB BAILOR 3B-SS-2B

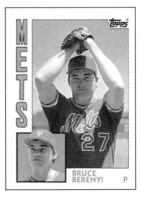
BRUCE BERENYI P

MARK BRADLEY OF

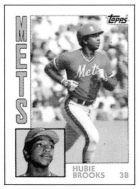
HUBIE BROOKS 3B

RON DARLING P

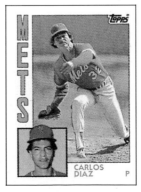
CARLOS DIAZ P

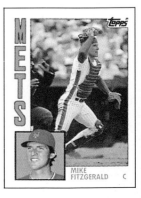
MIKE FITZGERALD C

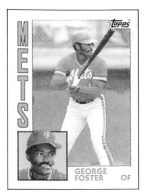
George Foster OF

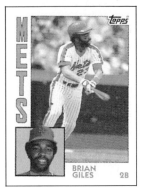
Brian Giles 2B

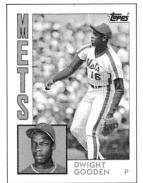
Dwight Gooden P

Tom Gorman P

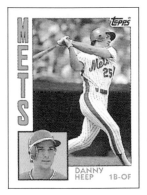
Danny Heep 1B-OF

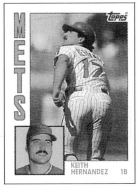
Keith Hernandez 1B

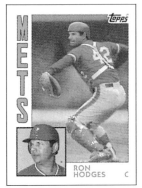
Ron Hodges C

Scott Holman P

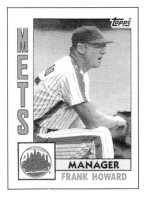
Manager Frank Howard

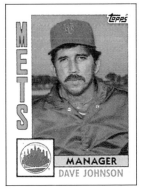
Manager Dave Johnson

Dave Kingman 1B

Ed Lynch P

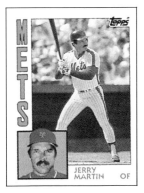
Jerry Martin OF

Jose Oquendo SS

Jesse Orosco P

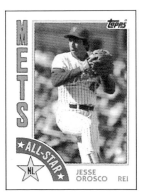
All-Star Jesse Orosco REI

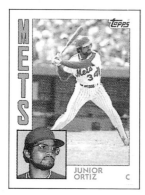

JUNIOR
ORTIZ          C

TOM
SEAVER        P

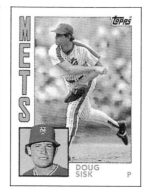

DOUG
SISK          P

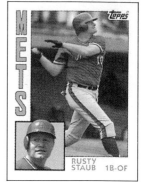

RUSTY
STAUB     1B-OF

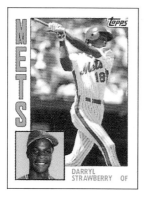

DARRYL
STRAWBERRY   OF

CRAIG
SWAN          P

WALT
TERRELL       P

MIKE
TORREZ        P

MOOKIE
WILSON        OF

METS
BATTING & PITCHING LEADERS

TOM SEAVER
3.55 ERA

MOOKIE WILSON
.276 BA

# 1985

Frank Cashen swung a masterful deal when he obtained Gary Carter, the best catcher in the N.L., from Montreal. The price was high (Hubie Brooks, Mike Fitzgerald and prospects Floyd Youmans and Herm Winningham), but worth it. Carter was a force behind the plate and hit .281 with 32 homers and 100 RBIs. He helped the Mets improve to 98-64, but it wasn't enough as the Cards (101-61) edged them for the division title by three games. The Mets had cut the deficit to one game with four left but lost 4-3 to the Cards. At age 20 Dwight Gooden was the best pitcher in the world. He became the youngest 20-game winner (24-4) of this century and the youngest Cy Young Award winner. The hard-throwing righthander with the outstanding curve led the N.L. in wins, ERA (1.53) and strikeouts (268). He set club records with eight shutouts and 14 consecutive victories. Ron Darling was lost in the Dr. K glitz at 16-6 with a 2.90 ERA. Keith Hernandez was magnificent again (.309, 91 RBIs, major league-record 24 game-winning RBIs, eighth straight Gold Glove). Darryl Strawberry, despite being sidelined seven weeks after tearing ligaments in his right thumb while diving for a fly ball, hit 29 homers with 79 RBIs in 111 games.

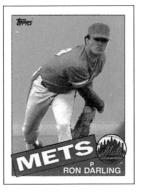

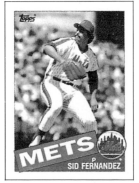

THE 1968 #1 DRAFT PICK

TIM FOLI
NEW YORK METS

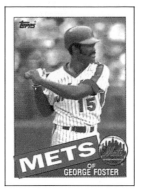

METS
OF
GEORGE FOSTER

METS
P
BRENT GAFF

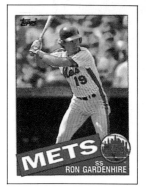

METS
SS
RON GARDENHIRE

DWIGHT GOODEN, Mets
Most Strikeouts, Rookie. Season

RECORD BREAKER

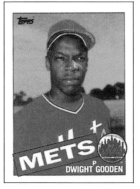

METS
P
DWIGHT GOODEN

METS
P
TOM GORMAN

METS
1B-OF
DANNY HEEP

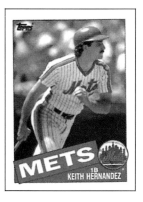

METS
1B
KEITH HERNANDEZ

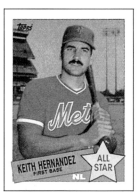

KEITH HERNANDEZ
FIRST BASE
ALL STAR
NL

METS
C
RON HODGES

METS MANAGER
DAVE JOHNSON

METS
3B-1B
RAY KNIGHT

METS
P
ED LYNCH

METS
OF
JERRY MARTIN

METS
SS
JOSE OQUENDO

JESSE OROSCO

JUNIOR ORTIZ

RAFAEL SANTANA

DOUG SISK

RUSTY STAUB

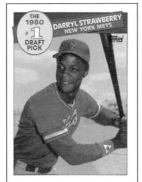

DARRYL STRAWBERRY

DARRYL STRAWBERRY

WALT TERRELL

MOOKIE WILSON

# 1986

They were called the Miracle Mets in 1969 when they won their first world championship. However, it wasn't until 17 years later that the Mets actually were blessed with a miracle — baseball version. In the World Series, they trailed the Red Sox three games to two and were down 5-3 with two outs and nobody on base in the bottom of the 10th inning of the sixth game. Then the Mets rose from the dead and won the game on singles by Gary Carter, Kevin Mitchell and Ray Knight, a wild pitch and an error. In the seventh game, they rallied from a 3-0 deficit to an electrifying 8-5 triumph. Amazing.

The Mets also won a heart-stopping, six-game playoff series over the Astros, winning the third game on centerfielder Lenny Dykstra's two-run homer in the ninth, winning the fifth game on Carter's single in the 12th and winning the sixth game in 16 innings after trailing 3-0 going into the ninth.

The regular season was nowhere as exhilarating as the Mets cakewalked to the N.L. East title. They started 20-4 and from July 1 on their lead was always in double figures. They celebrated their silver anniversary with a golden performance, going 108 – 54 and finishing 21½ games ahead of the Phils to break the win-margin record since division play began in 1969. Dykstra (.295, 31 steals) and second baseman Wally Backman (.320) were the tablesetters for Keith Hernandez (.310, 83 RBIs), Carter (24 homers, tied Rusty Staub's team record with 105 RBIs), Darryl Strawberry (27 homers, 93 RBIs) and Knight (.298, 76 RBIs). The Mets were the only team to have all five starting pitchers win in double figures with Bobby Ojeda (18-5, 2.57 ERA), obtained from Boston in the offseason, Dwight Gooden (17-6, 2.84, first pitcher to get 200 strikeouts in his first three seasons), Sid Fernandez (16-6, 3.52), Ron Darling (15-6, 2.81) and Rick Aguilera (10-7, 3.88).

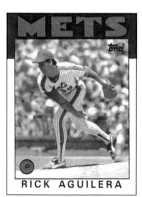
RICK AGUILERA

WALLY BACKMAN

BRUCE BERENYI

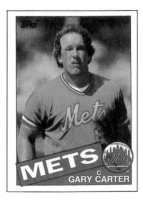
GARY CARTER

GARY CARTER

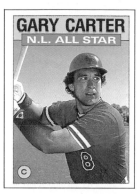

GARY CARTER
N.L. ALL STAR

KELVIN CHAPMAN

JOHN CHRISTENSEN

RON DARLING

LEN DYKSTRA

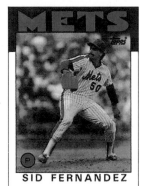

SID FERNANDEZ

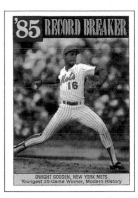

GEORGE FOSTER

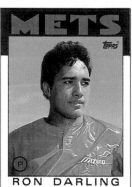

BRENT GAFF

RON GARDENHIRE

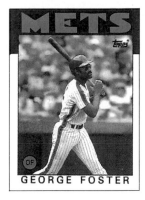

'85 RECORD BREAKER

DWIGHT GOODEN, NEW YORK METS
Youngest 20-Game Winner, Modern History

DWIGHT GOODEN

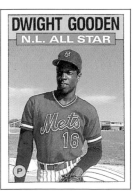

DWIGHT GOODEN
N.L. ALL STAR

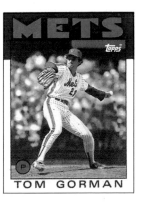

TOM GORMAN

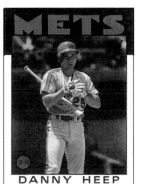

DANNY HEEP

'85 RECORD BREAKER

KEITH HERNANDEZ, NEW YORK METS
Most Game-Winning RBI, Season

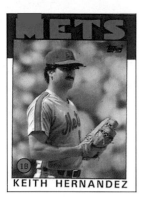

KEITH HERNANDEZ

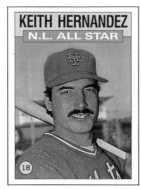

KEITH HERNANDEZ
N.L. ALL STAR

CLINT HURDLE

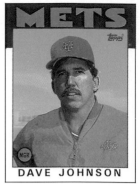

DAVE JOHNSON

METS
3B
HOWARD JOHNSON

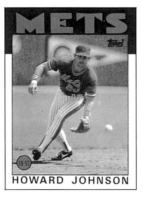

HOWARD JOHNSON

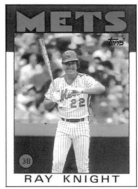

RAY KNIGHT

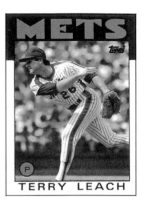

TERRY LEACH

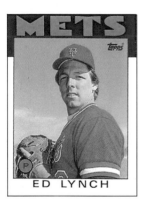

ED LYNCH

METS
ROGER McDOWELL

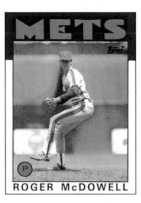

ROGER McDOWELL

JESSE OROSCO

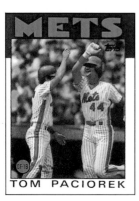

TOM PACIOREK

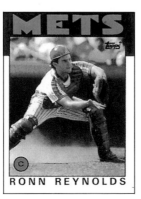

RONN REYNOLDS

METS
JOE SAMBITO

RAFAEL SANTANA

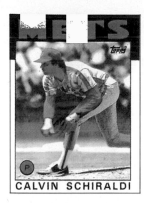

CALVIN SCHIRALDI

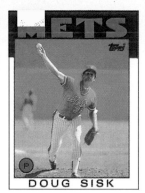

DOUG SISK

RUSTY STAUB

DARRYL STRAWBERRY

MOOKIE WILSON

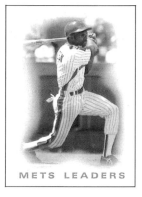

METS LEADERS

# 1987

When the 1987 season had run its ordained course, the Mets learned what the late Vince Lombardi meant when he said "Winning isn't everything, it's the only thing." Universally expected to repeat their 1986 Championship season, the Mets fell short by winning 92 games.

None of the club's regulars batted .300 and Dwight Gooden, who didn't pitch until June, was the staff's top winner with 15 victories. The pitching, with many on the staff sidelined at various times, was spotty. The bullpen duo of Roger McDowell and Jesse Orosco had their moments, but not often enough. Ron Darling and Sid Fernandez, each ended the year with 12-8 records. The righthander was out the final month with a thumb injury and earlier experienced a nine-week stretch during which he was 0-6 with eight no-decisions. The lefthanded Fernandez, 9-3 on June 21, won only three games the rest of the way and was bothered by a recurring shoulder ailment.

Switchhitting third baseman Howard Johnson emerged with 36 home runs and 99 RBI, while Darryl Strawberry enjoyed career highs in homers (39), RBIs (104) and stolen bases (36). Howard and Darryl also became the first pair of teammates to join the elite 30-30 club of 30 home runs and 30 stolen bases. Ho Jo was also the first infielder to reach this milestone. The Mets' future continued to brighten, however, as several of their quality minor leaguers gave indications they were on the verge of claiming varsity spots.

RICK AGUILERA

BILL ALMON

RICK ANDERSON

WALLY BACKMAN

BRUCE BERENYI

GARY CARTER

GARY CARTER
ALL-STAR

DAVE CONE

RON
DARLING

LEN
DYKSTRA

SID
FERNANDEZ

DWIGHT
GOODEN

DWIGHT
GOODEN

ALL STAR

ED HEARN

DANNY
HEEP

KEITH
HERNANDEZ

KEITH
HERNANDEZ

ALL STAR

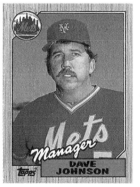

DAVE
JOHNSON

HOWARD
JOHNSON

RAY
KNIGHT

TERRY
LEACH

BARRY
LYONS

Future Stars
DAVE
MAGADAN

LEE
MAZZILLI

ROGER
McDOWELL

KEVIN
McREYNOLDS

JOHN
MITCHELL

KEVIN
MITCHELL

RANDY
MYERS

RANDY
NIEMANN

BOB
OJEDA

JESSE
OROSCO

RAFAEL
SANTANA

DOUG
SISK

DARRYL
STRAWBERRY

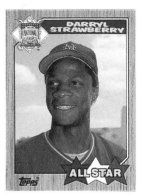

DARRYL
STRAWBERRY

ALL STAR

TIM
TEUFEL

MOOKIE
WILSON

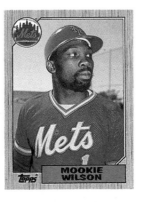

METS LEADERS

# 1988

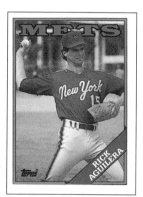

RICK AGUILERA

BILL ALMON

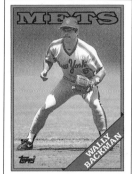

WALLY BACKMAN

JOHN CANDELARIA

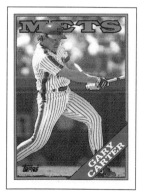

GARY CARTER

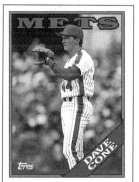

DAVE CONE

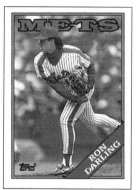

RON DARLING

LEN DYKSTRA

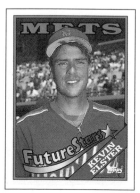

Future Stars

KEVIN ELSTER

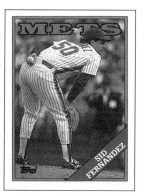

SID FERNANDEZ

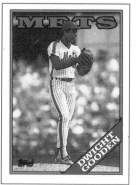

DWIGHT GOODEN

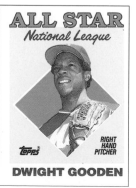

ALL STAR
*National League*

RIGHT
HAND
PITCHER

DWIGHT GOODEN

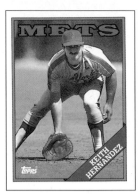

KEITH HERNANDEZ

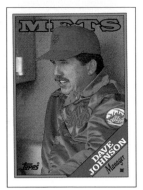

DAVE JOHNSON — Manager

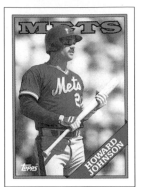

HOWARD JOHNSON

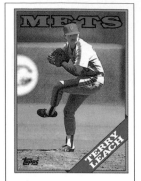

TERRY LEACH

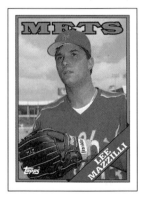

BARRY LYONS

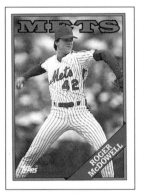

ROGER McDOWELL

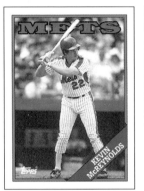

KEVIN McREYNOLDS

DAVE MAGADAN

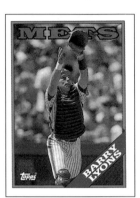

LEE MAZZILLI

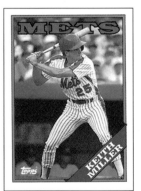

KEITH MILLER

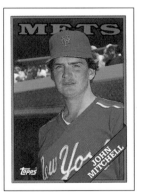

JOHN MITCHELL

RANDY MYERS

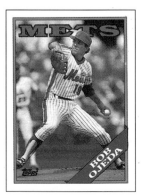

BOB OJEDA

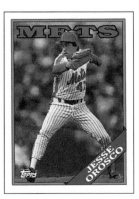

JESSE OROSCO

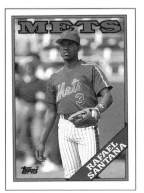

RAFAEL SANTANA

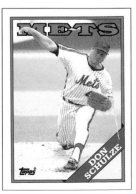

DON SCHULZE

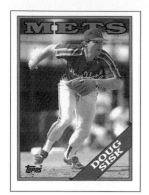

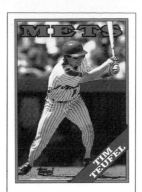

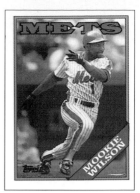

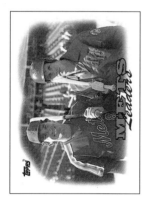

**1951:** Blue Back of Johnny Mize (50) lists for $25 . . . Red Back of Duke Snider (38) lists for $18 . . . Complete set of 9 Team Cards lists for $900 . . . Complete set of 11 Connie Mack All-Stars lists for $2750 with Babe Ruth and Lou Gehrig listing for $700 each . . . Current All-Stars of Jim Konstanty, Robin Roberts and Eddie Stanky list for $4000 each . . . Complete set lists for $14,250.

**1952:** Mickey Mantle (311) is unquestionably the most sought-after post-war gum card, reportedly valued at $6,500-plus . . . Ben Chapman (391) is photo of Sam Chapman . . . Complete set lists in excess of $36,000.

**1953:** Mickey Mantle (82) and Willie Mays (244) list for $1,500 each . . . Set features first TOPPS card of Hall-of-Famer Whitey Ford (207) and only TOPPS card of Hall-of-Famer Satchel Paige (220). Pete Runnels (219) is photo of Don Johnson . . . Complete set lists for $9,500.

**1954:** Ted Williams is depicted on two cards (1 and 250) . . . Set features rookie cards of Hank Aaron (128), Ernie Banks (94) and Al Kaline (201) . . . Card of Aaron lists for $650 . . . Card of Willie Mays (90) lists for $200 . . . Complete set lists for $5,500.

**1955:** Set features rookie cards of Sandy Koufax (123), Harmon Killebrew (124) and Roberto Clemente (164) . . . The Clemente and Willie Mays (194) cards list for $425 each . . .Complete set lists for $3,900.

**1956:** Set features rookie cards of Hall-of-Famers Will Harridge (1), Warren Giles (2), Walter Alston (8) and Luis Aparicio (292) . . . Card of Mickey Mantle (135) lists for $650 . . . Card of Willie Mays (130) lists for $125 . . . Complete set lists for $4,000 . . . The Team Cards are found both dated (1955) and undated and are valued at $15 (dated) and more . . . There are two unnumbered Checklist Cards valued high.

**1957:** Set features rookie cards of Don Drysdale (18), Frank Robinson (35) and Brooks Robinson (328) . . . A reversal of photo negative made Hank Aaron (20) appear as a left-handed batter . . . Card of Mickey Mantle (95) lists for $600 . . . Cards of Brooks Robinson and Sandy Koufax (302) list for $275 each . . . Complete set lists for $4,800.

**1958:** Set features first TOPPS cards of Casey Stengel (475) and Stan Musial (476) . . . Mike McCormick (37) is photo of Ray Monzant . . . Milt Bolling (188) is photo of Lou Berberet . . . Bob Smith (226) is photo of Bobby Gene Smith . . . Card of Mickey Mantle (150) lists for $400 . . . Card of Ted Williams (1) lists for $325 . . . Complete set lists for $4,800.

**1959:** In a notable error, Lou Burdette (440) is shown posing as a left-handed pitcher . . . Set features rookie card of Bob Gibson (514) . . . Ralph Lumenti (316) is photo of Camilo Pascual . . . Card of Gibson lists for $200 . . . Card of Mickey Mantle (10) lists for $300 . . . Complete set lists for $3,000.

**1960:** A run of 32 consecutively numbered rookie cards (117-148) includes the first card of Carl Yastrzemski (148) . . . J.C. Martin (346) is photo of Gary Peters . . . Gary Peters (407) is photo of J.C. Martin . . . Card of Yastrzemski lists for $150 . . . Card of Mickey Mantle (350) lists for $300 . . . Complete set lists for $2,600.

**1961:** The Warren Spahn All-Star (589) should have been numbered 587 . . . Set features rookie cards of Billy Williams (141) and Juan Marichal (417) . . . Dutch Dotterer (332) is photo of his brother, Tommy . . . Card of Mickey Mantle (300) lists for $200 . . . Card of Carl Yastrzemski (287) lists for $90 . . . Complete set lists for $3,600.

**1962:** Set includes special Babe Ruth feature (135-144) . . . some Hal Reniff cards numbered 139 should be 159 . . . Set features rookie card of Lou Brock (387) . . . Gene Freese (205) is shown posing as a left-handed batter . . . Card of Mickey Mantle (200) lists for $325 . . . Card of Carl Yastrzemski (425) lists for $125 . . . Complete set lists for $3,300.

**1963:** Set features rookie card of Pete Rose (537), which lists for $500-plus . . . Bob Uecker (126) is shown posing as a left-handed batter . . . Don Landrum (113) is photo of Ron Santo . . . Eli Grba (231) is photo of Ryne Duren . . . Card of Mickey Mantle (200) lists for $200 . . . Card of Lou Brock (472) lists for $75 . . . Complete set lists for $2,900.

**1964:** Set features rookie cards of Richie Allen (243), Tony Conigliaro (287) and Phil Niekro (541) . . . Lou Burdette is again shown posing as a left-handed pitcher . . . Bud Bloomfield (532) is photo of Jay Ward . . . Card of Pete Rose (125) lists for $150 . . . Card of Mickey Mantle (50) lists for $175 . . . Complete set lists for $1,600.

**1965:** Set features rookie cards of Dave Johnson (473), Steve Carlton (477) and Jim Hunter (526) . . . Lew Krausse (462) is photo of Pete Lovrich . . . Gene Freese (492) is again shown posing as a left-handed batter . . . Cards of Carlton and Pete Rose (207) list for $135 . . . Card of Mickey Mantle (350) lists for $300 . . . Complete set lists for $800.

**1966:** Set features rookie card of Jim Palmer (126) . . . For the third time (see 1962 and 1965) Gene Freese (319) is shown posing as a left-handed batter . . . Dick Ellsworth (447) is photo of Ken Hubbs (died February 13, 1964) . . . Card of Gaylord Perry (598) lists for $175 . . . Card of Willie McCovey (550) lists for $80 . . . Complete set lists for $2,500.

**1967:** Set features rookie cards of Rod Carew (569) and Tom Seaver (581) . . . Jim Fregosi (385) is shown posing as a left-handed batter . . . George Korince (72) is photo of James Brown but was later corrected on a second Korince card (526) . . . Card of Carew lists for $150 . . . Card of Maury Wills (570) lists for $65 . . . Complete set lists for $2,500.

**1968:** Set features rookie cards of Nolan Ryan (177) and Johnny Bench (247) . . . The special feature of The Sporting News All-Stars (361-380) includes eight players in the Hall of Fame . . . Card of Ryan lists for $135 . . . Card of Bench lists for $125 . . . Complete set lists for $1,200.

**1969:** Set features rookie card of Reggie Jackson (260) . . . There are two poses each for Clay Dalrymple (151) and Donn Clendenon (208) . . . Aurelio Rodriguez (653) is photo of Lenny Garcia (Angels' bat boy) . . . Card of Mickey Mantle (500) lists for $150 . . . Card of Jackson lists for $175 . . . Complete set lists for $1,200.

**1970:** Set features rookie cards of Vida Blue (21), Thurman Munson (189) and Bill Buckner (286) . . . Also included are two deceased players Miguel Fuentes (88) and Paul Edmondson (414) who died after cards went to press . . . Card of Johnny Bench (660) lists for $75 . . . Card of Pete Rose (580) lists for $75 . . . Complete set lists for $1,000.

**1971:** Set features rookie card of Steve Garvey (341) . . . the final series (644-752) is found in lesser quantity and includes rookie card (664) of three pitchers named Reynolds (Archie, Bob and Ken) . . . Card of Garvey lists for $65 . . . Card of Pete Rose (100) lists for $45 . . . Complete set lists for $1,000.

**1972:** There were 16 cards featuring photos of players in their boyhood years . . . Dave Roberts (91) is photo of Danny Coombs . . . Brewers Rookie Card (162) includes photos of Darrell Porter and Jerry Bell, which were reversed . . . Cards of Steve Garvey (686) and Rod Carew (695) list for $60 . . . Card of Pete Rose (559) lists for $50 . . . Complete set lists for $1,000.

**1973:** A special Home Run Card (1) depicted Babe Ruth, Hank Aaron and Willie Mays . . . Set features rookie card of Mike Schmidt (615) listing for $175 . . . Joe Rudi (360) is photo of Gene Tenace . . . Card of Pete Rose (130) lists for $18 . . . Card of Reggie Jackson (255) lists for $12.50 . . . Complete set lists for $600.

**1974:** Set features 15 San Diego Padres cards printed as "Washington, N.L." due to report of franchise move, later corrected . . . Also included was a 44-card Traded Series which updated team changes . . . Set features rookie card of Dave Winfield (456) . . . Card of Mike Schmidt (283) lists for $35 . . . Card of Winfield lists for $25 . . . Complete set lists for $325.

**1975:** Herb Washington (407) is the only card ever published with position "designated runner," featuring only base-running statistics . . . Set features rookie cards of Robin Yount (223), George Brett (228), Jim Rice (616), Gary Carter (620) and Keith Hernandez (623) . . . Don Wilson (455) died after cards went to press (January 5, 1975) . . . Card of Brett lists for $50 . . . Cards of Rice and Carter list for $35 . . . Complete set lists for $475 . . . TOPPS also tested the complete 660-card series in a smaller size (2¼" x 3 1/8") in certain areas of USA in a limited supply . . . Complete set of "Mini-Cards" lists for $700.

**1976:** As in 1974 there was a 44-card Traded Series . . . Set features five Father & Son cards (66-70) and ten All-Time All-Stars (341-350) . . . Card of Pete Rose (240) lists for $15 . . . Cards of Jim Rice (340), Gary Carter (441) and George Brett (19) list for $12 . . . Complete set lists for $225.

**1977:** Set features rookie cards of Andre Dawson (473) and Dale Murphy (476) . . . Reuschel Brother Combination (634) shows the two (Paul and Rick) misidentified . . . Dave Collins (431) is photo of Bob Jones . . . Card of Murphy lists for $65 . . . Card of Pete Rose (450) lists for $8.50 . . . Complete set lists for $250.

**1978:** Record Breakers (1-7) feature Lou Brock, Sparky Lyle, Willie McCovey, Brooks Robinson, Pete Rose, Nolan Ryan and Reggie Jackson . . . Set features rookie cards of Jack Morris (703), Lou Whitaker (704), Paul Molitor/Alan Trammell (707), Lance Parrish (708) and Eddie Murray (36) . . . Card of Murray lists for $35 . . . Card of Parrish lists for $35 . . . Complete set lists for $200.

**1979:** Bump Wills (369) was originally shown with Blue Jays affiliation but later corrected to Rangers . . . Set features rookie cards of Ozzie Smith (116), Pedro Guerrero (719), Lonnie Smith (722) and Terry Kennedy (724) . . . Larry Cox (489) is photo of Dave Rader . . . Card of Dale Murphy (39) lists for $8 . . . Cards of Ozzie Smith and Eddie Murray (640) list for $7.50 . . . Complete set lists for $135.

**1980:** Highlights (1-6) feature Hall-of-Famers Lou Brock, Carl Yastrzemski, Willie McCovey and Pete Rose . . . Set features rookie cards of Dave Stieb (77), Rickey Henderson (482) and Dan Quisenberry (667) . . . Card of Henderson lists for $28 . . . Card of Dale Murphy (274) lists for $5.50 . . . Complete set lists for $135.

**1981:** Set features rookie cards of Fernando Valenzuela (302), Kirk Gibson (315), Harold Baines (347) and Tim Raines (479) . . . Jeff Cox (133) is photo of Steve McCatty . . . John Littlefield (489) is photo of Mark Riggins . . . Card of Valenzuela lists for $7.50 . . . Card of Raines lists for $9 . . . Complete set lists for $80.

**1982:** Pascual Perez (383) printed with no position on front lists for $35, later corrected . . . Set features rookie cards of Cal Ripken (21), Jesse Barfield (203), Steve Sax (681) and Kent Hrbek (766) . . . Dave Rucker (261) is photo of Roger Weaver . . . Steve Bedrosian (502) is photo of Larry Owen . . . Card of Ripken lists for $12.50 . . . Cards of Barfield and Sax list for $5 . . . Complete set lists for $75.

**1983:** Record Breakers (1-6) feature Tony Armas, Rickey Henderson, Greg Minton, Lance Parrish, Manny Trillo and John Wathan . . . A series of Super Veterans features early and current photos of 34 leading players . . . Set features rookie cards of Tony Gwynn (482) and Wade Boggs (498) . . . Card of Boggs lists for $32 . . . Card of Gwynn lists for $16 . . . Complete set lists for $85.

**1984:** Highlights (1-6) salute eleven different players . . . A parade of superstars is included in Active Leaders (701-718) . . . Set features rookie card of Don Mattingly (8) listing for $35 . . . Card of Darryl Strawberry (182) lists for $10 . . . Complete set lists for $85.

**1985:** A Father & Son Feature (131-143) is again included . . . Set features rookie cards of Scott Bankhead (393), Mike Dunne (395), Shane Mack (398), John Marzano (399), Oddibe McDowell (400), Mark McGwire (401), Pat Pacillo (402), Cory Snyder (403) and Billy Swift (404) as part of salute to 1984 USA Baseball Team (389-404) that participated in Olympic Games plus rookie cards of Roger Clemens (181) and Eric Davis (627) . . . Card of McGwire lists for $20 . . . Card of Davis lists for $18 . . . Card of Clemens lists for $11 . . . Complete set lists for $95.

**1986:** Set includes Pete Rose Feature (2-7), which reproduces each of Rose's TOPPS cards from 1963 thru 1985 (four per card) . . . Bob Rodgers (141) should have been numbered 171 . . . Ryne Sandberg (690) is the only card with TOPPS logo omitted . . . Complete set lists for $24.

**1987:** Record Breakers (1-7) feature Roger Clemens, Jim Deshaies, Dwight Evans, Davey Lopes, Dave Righetti, Ruben Sierra and Todd Worrell . . . Jim Gantner (108) is shown with Brewers logo reversed . . . Complete set lists for $22.

**1988:** Record Breakers (1-7) include Vince Coleman, Don Mattingly, Mark McGwire, Eddie Murray, Phil & Joe Niekro, Nolan Ryan and Benny Santiago. Al Leiter (18) was originally shown with photo of minor leaguer Steve George and later corrected. Complete set lists for $20.00.

# Pitching Record & Index

| PLAYER | G | IP | W | L | R | ER | SO | BB | GS | CG | SHO | SV | ERA |
|---|---|---|---|---|---|---|---|---|---|---|---|---|---|
| AGUILERA, RICK | 49 | 264 | 20 | 14 | 119 | 105 | 178 | 73 | 39 | 4 | | 0 | 3.58 |
| AKER, JACK | 495 | 746 | 47 | 45 | | | 404 | 274 | 0 | 0 | | 123 | 3.28 |
| ALLEN, NEIL | 367 | 793.2 | 53 | 58 | 356 | 322 | 508 | 344 | 46 | 7 | 5 | 75 | 3.65 |
| ANDERSON, CRAIG | 82 | 192 | 7 | 23 | | | 94 | 81 | 17 | 2 | 0 | 5 | 5.11 |
| ANDERSON, RICK | 15 | 49.2 | 2 | 1 | 17 | 15 | 21 | 11 | 5 | 0 | 0 | 0 | 2.72 |
| APODACA, BOB | 184 | 362 | 16 | 25 | | | 197 | 131 | 11 | 1 | 0 | 26 | 2.86 |
| ARRIGO, GERRY | 194 | 620 | 35 | 40 | | | 433 | 291 | 80 | 9 | 3 | 4 | 4.14 |
| BALDWIN, RICK | 105 | 183 | 4 | 7 | | | 86 | 75 | 0 | 0 | 0 | 7 | 3.59 |
| BAMBERGER, GEORGE | 10 | 14 | 0 | 0 | | | 3 | 10 | 1 | 0 | 0 | 1 | 9.64 |
| BAUTA, ED | 97 | 149 | 6 | 6 | | | 89 | 70 | 0 | 0 | 0 | 11 | 4.35 |
| BEARNARTH, LARRY | 173 | 323 | 13 | 21 | | | 124 | 135 | 7 | 0 | 0 | 8 | 4.12 |
| BENNETT, DENNIS | 182 | 863 | 43 | 47 | | | 572 | 281 | 127 | 28 | 6 | 6 | 3.69 |
| BERENGUER, JUAN | 183 | 645 | 30 | 41 | 324 | 287 | 498 | 335 | 86 | 5 | 2 | 5 | 4.00 |
| BERENYI, BRUCE | 142 | 782 | 44 | 55 | 392 | 350 | 607 | 425 | 131 | 13 | 3 | 0 | 4.03 |
| BERNARD, DWIGHT | 115 | 176 | 4 | 8 | | | 92 | 86 | 2 | 0 | 0 | 6 | 4.14 |
| BETHKE, JIM | 25 | 40 | 2 | 0 | | | 19 | 22 | 0 | 0 | 0 | 0 | 4.28 |
| BOITANO, DANNY | 51 | 71.1 | 2 | 2 | | | 52 | 28 | 0 | 0 | 0 | 0 | 5.68 |
| BOMBACK, MARK | 74 | 314.2 | 16 | 18 | | | 124 | 110 | 45 | 2 | 1 | 0 | 4.46 |
| BRUHERT, MIKE | 27 | 134 | 4 | 11 | | | 56 | 34 | 22 | 1 | 0 | 0 | 4.77 |
| BURRIS, RAY | 447 | 2083.2 | 102 | 127 | | | 1023 | 477 | 290 | 47 | 10 | 4 | 4.10 |
| CANDELARIA, JOHN | 350 | 2016.2 | 141 | 89 | 775 | 698 | 1276 | 300 | 300 | 47 | 11 | 15 | 3.12 |
| CAPRA, BUZZ | 142 | 543 | 31 | 37 | | | 362 | 258 | 61 | 16 | 5 | 5 | 3.88 |
| CARDWELL, DON | 410 | 2122 | 102 | 138 | | | 1211 | 671 | 301 | 72 | 17 | 7 | 3.92 |
| CHANCE, DEAN | 406 | 2148 | 128 | 115 | | | 1534 | 739 | 294 | 83 | 33 | 23 | 2.92 |
| CISCO, GALEN | 192 | 658 | 25 | 56 | | | 325 | 281 | 78 | 9 | 3 | 2 | 4.57 |
| CONNORS, BILL | 26 | 43 | 0 | 2 | | | 24 | 19 | 1 | 0 | 0 | 0 | 7.53 |
| CRAIG, ROGER | 368 | 1537 | 74 | 98 | | | 803 | 522 | 186 | 58 | 7 | 19 | 3.82 |
| CRAM, JERRY | 23 | 48 | 0 | 3 | | | 22 | 13 | 2 | 0 | 0 | 3 | 3.00 |
| DARLING, RON | 108 | 726 | 44 | 24 | | | 510 | 316 | 107 | 11 | 2 | 0 | 3.12 |
| DENEHY, BILL | 49 | 105 | 1 | 10 | | | 63 | 61 | 10 | 1 | 0 | 1 | 4.54 |
| DIAZ, CARLOS | 160 | 232.2 | 13 | 6 | | | 189 | 90 | 4 | 0 | 0 | 4 | 3.09 |
| DILAURO, JACK | 65 | 98 | 2 | 7 | | | 50 | 35 | 4 | 0 | 0 | 2 | 3.03 |
| DILLON, STEVE | 3 | 5 | 0 | 0 | | | 3 | 2 | 0 | 0 | 0 | 0 | 9.00 |
| EILERS, DAVE | 81 | 124 | 8 | 6 | | | 52 | 29 | 0 | 0 | 0 | 3 | 4.43 |
| ELLIS, DOCK | 345 | 2129 | 138 | 119 | | | 1136 | 674 | 317 | 71 | 14 | 0 | 3.45 |
| ESPINOSA, NINO | 139 | 820 | 44 | 55 | | | 338 | 252 | 130 | 24 | 5 | 0 | 4.16 |
| ESTRADA, CHUCK | 146 | 764 | 50 | 44 | 285 | 252 | 535 | 416 | 105 | 24 | 7 | 2 | 4.08 |
| FALCONE, PETE | 325 | 1434. | 70 | 90 | | | 865 | 671 | 217 | 25 | 7 | 1 | 4.07 |
| FERNANDEZ, SID | 75 | 470.2 | 31 | 22 | 182 | 172 | 451 | 212 | 73 | 5 | 1 | 0 | 3.29 |
| FISHER, JACK | 400 | 1977 | 86 | 139 | | | 1017 | 605 | 265 | 62 | 9 | 1 | 4.06 |
| FOLKERS, RICH | 195 | 422 | 19 | 23 | | | 242 | 170 | 27 | 2 | 0 | 9 | 4.12 |
| FRIEND, BOB | 602 | 3612 | 197 | 230 | | | 1734 | 894 | 497 | 163 | 36 | 11 | 3.58 |
| FRISELLA, DANNY | 351 | 601 | 34 | 40 | | | 471 | 286 | 17 | 0 | 0 | 57 | 3.37 |
| GAFF, BRENT | 58 | 126.1 | 4 | 5 | | | 60 | 47 | 5 | 0 | 0 | 2 | 4.06 |
| GARDNER, ROB | 109 | 332 | 14 | 18 | | | 193 | 133 | 42 | 4 | 0 | 2 | 4.34 |
| GENTRY, GARY | 157 | 903 | 46 | 49 | | | 615 | 369 | 138 | 25 | 8 | 1 | 3.56 |
| GIBSON, BOB L. | 86 | 242 | 11 | 16 | | | 153 | 142 | 17 | 1 | 0 | 13 | 4.20 |
| GLYNN, ED | 172 | 263 | 12 | 17 | | | 181 | 147 | 8 | 0 | 0 | 12 | 4.11 |
| GOODEN, DWIGHT | 99 | 744.2 | 58 | 19 | 215 | 189 | 744 | 222 | 99 | 35 | 13 | 0 | 2.28 |
| GORMAN, TOM P. | 112 | 149.1 | 9 | 9 | | | 128 | 56 | 7 | 0 | 0 | 0 | 4.15 |
| GREEN, DALLAS | 185 | 562 | 20 | 22 | | | 268 | 197 | 46 | 12 | 2 | 4 | 4.26 |
| GRZENDA, JOE | 219 | 309 | 14 | 13 | | | 173 | 120 | 3 | 0 | 0 | 14 | 3.99 |
| HALL, TOM | 358 | 854 | 52 | 33 | | | 797 | 382 | 63 | 7 | 3 | 32 | 3.27 |
| HAMILTON, JACK | 218 | 612 | 32 | 40 | | | 357 | 238 | 65 | 8 | 2 | 20 | 4.53 |
| HARRIS, GREG | 216 | 440 | 22 | 25 | | | 373 | 178 | 25 | 1 | 1 | 35 | 3.42 |
| HASSLER, ANDY | 377 | 1113 | 44 | 70 | 188 | 167 | 625 | 516 | 112 | 26 | 5 | 29 | 3.85 |

| PLAYER | G | IP | W | L | R | ER | SO | BB | GS | CG | SHO | SV | ERA |
|---|---|---|---|---|---|---|---|---|---|---|---|---|---|
| HAUSMAN, TOM | 160 | 441.1 | 15 | 23 | | | 180 | 121 | 33 | 2 | 0 | 3 | 3.79 |
| HENDLEY, BOB | 216 | 879 | 48 | 52 | | | 522 | 329 | 126 | 25 | 6 | 12 | 3.97 |
| HENNIGAN, PHIL | 176 | 280 | 17 | 14 | | | 188 | 133 | 2 | 0 | 0 | 26 | 4.27 |
| HEPLER, BILL | 37 | 69 | 2 | 3 | | | 25 | 51 | 3 | 0 | 0 | 0 | 3.52 |
| HERBEL, RON | 331 | 895 | 42 | 37 | | | 447 | 285 | 79 | 11 | 3 | 16 | 3.82 |
| HILLMAN, DAVE | 188 | 624 | 21 | 37 | | | 296 | 185 | 64 | 8 | 1 | 0 | 3.87 |
| HINSLEY, JERRY | 11 | 20 | 0 | 2 | | | 14 | 11 | 2 | 0 | 0 | 0 | 7.20 |
| HOLMAN, SCOTT | 43 | 134.2 | 3 | 8 | | | 58 | 60 | 14 | 1 | 0 | 0 | 3.34 |
| HOOK, JAY | 160 | 754 | 29 | 62 | | | 394 | 275 | 112 | 30 | 2 | 1 | 5.22 |
| HUDSON, JESSIE | 1 | 2 | 0 | 0 | | | 3 | 2 | 1 | 0 | 0 | 0 | 4.50 |
| JACKSON, AL | 302 | 1389 | 67 | 99 | | | 738 | 407 | 184 | 54 | 14 | 10 | 3.98 |
| JACKSON, ROY LEE | 280 | 559.1 | 28 | 34 | | | 351 | 203 | 18 | 0 | 0 | 34 | 3.77 |
| JOHNSON, BOB D. | 183 | 693 | 28 | 34 | | | 507 | 269 | 76 | 18 | 2 | 12 | 3.48 |
| JONES, RANDY | 305 | 1931.2 | 100 | 123 | | | 735 | 503 | 285 | 73 | 19 | 0 | 3.42 |
| JONES, SHERMAN | 48 | 110 | 2 | 6 | | | 53 | 46 | 5 | 0 | 0 | 3 | 4.75 |
| KOBEL, KEVIN | 115 | 475 | 18 | 34 | | | 205 | 152 | 64 | 5 | 3 | 0 | 3.88 |
| KOONCE, CAL | 334 | 972 | 47 | 49 | | | 504 | 368 | 90 | 9 | 3 | 24 | 3.78 |
| KOOSMAN, JERRY | 612 | 3839.1 | 222 | 209 | | | 2556 | 1198 | 527 | 140 | 33 | 17 | 3.36 |
| KROLL, GARY | 71 | 160 | 6 | 7 | | | 138 | 91 | 13 | 1 | 0 | 2 | 4.22 |
| LABINE, CLEM | 513 | 1080 | 77 | 56 | | | 551 | 396 | 38 | 7 | 2 | 96 | 3.63 |
| LAMABE, JACK | 285 | 710 | 33 | 41 | | | 434 | 238 | 49 | 7 | 3 | 15 | 4.25 |
| LARY, FRANK | 350 | 2162 | 128 | 116 | | | 1099 | 616 | 292 | 126 | 21 | 11 | 3.49 |
| LEACH, TERRY | 64 | 136 | 6 | 6 | | | 76 | 44 | 2 | 0 | 0 | 4 | 3.24 |
| LEARY, TIM | 61 | 288 | 17 | 20 | | | 180 | 84 | 45 | 4 | 2 | 0 | 4.09 |
| LOCKE, RON | 25 | 41 | 1 | 2 | | | 17 | 22 | 3 | 0 | 0 | 0 | 3.51 |
| LOCKWOOD, SKIP | 420 | 1236 | 57 | 97 | | | 829 | 490 | 106 | 16 | 5 | 68 | 3.55 |
| LOLICH, MICKEY | 586 | 3640 | 217 | 191 | | | 2832 | 1099 | 496 | 195 | 41 | 6 | 3.44 |
| LYNCH, ED | 190 | 829.1 | 45 | 45 | | | 316 | 181 | 111 | 8 | 2 | 6 | 3.82 |
| MACKENZIE, KEN | 129 | 207 | 8 | 10 | | | 142 | 63 | 1 | 0 | 0 | 4 | 4.83 |
| MARSHALL, MIKE G. | 723 | 1386 | 97 | 112 | | | 880 | 514 | 24 | 3 | 1 | 187 | 3.15 |
| MATLACK, JON | 361 | 2363 | 125 | 126 | | | 1516 | 638 | 318 | 97 | 30 | 3 | 3.18 |
| McANDREW, JIM | 161 | 771 | 37 | 53 | | | 424 | 213 | 110 | 20 | 6 | 4 | 3.65 |
| McDOWELL, ROGER | 137 | 255.1 | 20 | 14 | 91 | 83 | 135 | 79 | 2 | 0 | 0 | 39 | 2.93 |
| McGRAW, TUG | 824 | 1515.2 | 96 | 92 | | | 1109 | 582 | 39 | 5 | 1 | 180 | 3.14 |
| MEDICH, GEORGE | 312 | 1995.2 | 124 | 105 | | | 955 | 624 | 287 | 71 | 16 | 2 | 3.78 |
| METZGER, BUTCH | 191 | 293 | 18 | 9 | | | 175 | 140 | 1 | 0 | 0 | 23 | 3.75 |
| MILLER, BOB G. | 86 | 189 | 6 | 8 | | | 75 | 92 | 8 | 1 | 0 | 1 | 4.71 |
| MILLER, BOB L. | 694 | 1552 | 69 | 81 | | | 895 | 608 | 99 | 7 | 0 | 52 | 3.37 |
| MILLER, DYAR | 251 | 466 | 23 | 17 | | | 235 | 177 | 1 | 0 | 0 | 32 | 3.23 |
| MILLER, LARRY | 48 | 145 | 5 | 14 | | | 93 | 57 | 20 | 1 | 0 | 0 | 4.72 |
| MIZELL, WILMER | 268 | 1528 | 90 | 88 | | | 918 | 680 | 230 | 61 | 15 | 0 | 3.85 |
| MOFORD, HERB | 50 | 158 | 5 | 13 | | | 78 | 64 | 14 | 6 | 0 | 3 | 5.01 |
| MOORHEAD, BOB | 47 | 119 | 0 | 7 | | | 68 | 47 | 7 | 0 | 0 | 3 | 4.54 |
| MURRAY, DALE | 514 | 898 | 53 | 50 | | | 400 | 329 | 1 | 0 | 0 | 60 | 3.82 |
| MYERS, RANDY | 11 | 12.2 | 0 | 0 | 5 | 5 | 15 | 10 | 0 | 0 | 0 | 0 | 3.55 |
| MYRICK, BOB | 82 | 140 | 3 | 6 | | | 73 | 59 | 5 | 0 | 0 | 1 | 3.47 |
| NIEMANN, RANDY | 116 | 194.2 | 6 | 8 | 107 | 98 | 101 | 75 | 10 | 0 | 0 | 3 | 4.53 |
| OJEDA, BOB | 172 | 935.2 | 62 | 44 | 435 | 398 | 573 | 337 | 143 | 27 | 7 | 1 | 3.83 |
| OROSCO, JESSE | 314 | 518.1 | 44 | 38 | 166 | 143 | 428 | 209 | 4 | 0 | 0 | 91 | 2.48 |
| OWNBEY, RICK | 22 | 104 | 2 | 8 | | | 58 | 72 | 16 | 2 | 0 | 0 | 4.24 |
| PACELLA, JOHN | 69 | 180.1 | 4 | 10 | | | 111 | 120 | 21 | 0 | 0 | 0 | 5.84 |
| PARKER, HARRY | 134 | 315 | 15 | 21 | | | 172 | 128 | 30 | 1 | 0 | 12 | 3.86 |
| PARSONS, TOM | 40 | 114 | 2 | 13 | | | 70 | 25 | 14 | 2 | 1 | 1 | 4.74 |
| POWELL, GROVER | 20 | 50 | 1 | 1 | | | 39 | 32 | 4 | 1 | 1 | 0 | 2.70 |
| PULEO, CHARLIE | 72 | 349.2 | 16 | 23 | | | 183 | 204 | 53 | 1 | 1 | 1 | 4.56 |
| RENIFF, HAL | 276 | 470 | 21 | 23 | | | 314 | 242 | 0 | 0 | 0 | 45 | 3.27 |

| PLAYER | G | IP | W | L | R | ER | SO | BB | GS | CG | SHO | SV | ERA |
|---|---|---|---|---|---|---|---|---|---|---|---|---|---|
| RIBANT, DENNIS | 149 | 519 | 24 | 29 | | | 241 | 126 | 56 | 12 | 2 | 9 | 3.87 |
| RICHARDSON, GORDON | 69 | 118 | 6 | 6 | | | 86 | 37 | 7 | 1 | 0 | 4 | 4.04 |
| ROBERTS, DAVE A. | 445 | 2098 | 103 | 125 | | | 957 | 615 | 277 | 77 | 20 | 15 | 3.78 |
| ROHR, LES | 6 | 24 | 2 | 3 | | | 20 | 17 | 4 | 0 | 0 | 0 | 3.75 |
| ROSE, DON | 19 | 46 | 1 | 4 | | | 40 | 20 | 4 | 0 | 0 | 0 | 4.11 |
| ROWE, DON | 26 | 55 | 0 | 0 | | | 27 | 21 | 1 | 0 | 0 | 0 | 4.25 |
| RYAN, NOLAN | 611 | 4115.1 | 253 | 226 | 1643 | 1440 | 4277 | 2268 | 577 | 203 | 54 | 3 | 3.15 |
| SADECKI, RAY | 563 | 2500 | 135 | 131 | | | 1614 | 922 | 327 | 85 | 20 | 7 | 3.78 |
| SAMBITO, JOE | 414 | 590.2 | 35 | 32 | 212 | 183 | 454 | 179 | 5 | 1 | 1 | 84 | 2.79 |
| SANDERS, KEN | 408 | 657 | 29 | 45 | | | 360 | 258 | 1 | 0 | 0 | 86 | 2.97 |
| SCARCE, MAC | 159 | 210 | 6 | 19 | | | 164 | 117 | 0 | 0 | 0 | 21 | 3.69 |
| SCHIRALDI, CALVIN | 40 | 94.2 | 6 | 5 | 48 | 45 | 92 | 36 | 7 | 0 | 0 | 9 | 4.28 |
| SCHULZE, DON | 62 | 281.2 | 11 | 21 | 191 | 171 | 119 | 88 | 49 | 4 | 0 | 0 | 5.46 |
| SCOTT, MIKE | 212 | 1160 | 65 | 62 | 541 | 477 | 750 | 363 | 185 | 16 | 10 | 3 | 3.70 |
| SEARAGE, RAY | 126 | 164.1 | 5 | 6 | 66 | 62 | 117 | 85 | 0 | 0 | 0 | 9 | 3.40 |
| SEAVER, TOM | 656 | 4782 | 311 | 205 | 1674 | 1511 | 3640 | 1390 | 647 | 231 | 61 | 1 | 2.84 |
| SELMA, DICK | 307 | 841 | 42 | 54 | | | 681 | 381 | 76 | 11 | 6 | 31 | 3.62 |
| SHAW, BOB | 430 | 1779 | 108 | 98 | | | 880 | 511 | 223 | 55 | 15 | 32 | 3.52 |
| SHAW, DON | 138 | 188 | 13 | 14 | | | 123 | 101 | 1 | 0 | 0 | 6 | 4.02 |
| SHORT, BILL | 73 | 131 | 5 | 11 | | | 71 | 64 | 16 | 3 | 1 | 2 | 4.74 |
| SIEBERT, PAUL | 87 | 129 | 3 | 8 | | | 59 | 73 | 7 | 1 | 1 | 3 | 3.77 |
| SISK, DOUG | 208 | 334.1 | 14 | 15 | 142 | 112 | 126 | 188 | 0 | 0 | 0 | 30 | 3.01 |
| SPAHN, WARREN | 750 | 5246 | 363 | 245 | | | 2583 | 1434 | 665 | 382 | 63 | 29 | 3.08 |
| STALLARD, TRACY | 183 | 765 | 30 | 57 | | | 477 | 343 | 104 | 21 | 3 | 4 | 4.16 |
| STONE, GEORGE | 203 | 1020 | 60 | 57 | | | 590 | 270 | 145 | 24 | 5 | 5 | 3.89 |
| STROHMAYER, JOHN | 142 | 313 | 11 | 9 | | | 200 | 128 | 17 | 2 | 0 | 4 | 4.46 |
| STROM, BRENT | 100 | 501 | 22 | 39 | | | 278 | 180 | 75 | 16 | 3 | 0 | 3.95 |
| STURDIVANT, TOM | 335 | 1136 | 59 | 51 | | | 704 | 449 | 101 | 22 | 7 | 17 | 3.75 |
| SUTHERLAND, DARRELL | 62 | 122 | 5 | 4 | | | 50 | 58 | 6 | 0 | 0 | 1 | 4.80 |
| SWAN, CRAIG | 231 | 1234.1 | 59 | 72 | | | 673 | 368 | 185 | 25 | 7 | 2 | 3.75 |
| TATE, RANDY | 26 | 138 | 5 | 13 | | | 99 | 86 | 23 | 2 | 0 | 0 | 4.43 |
| TAYLOR, CHUCK | 305 | 607 | 28 | 20 | | | 282 | 162 | 21 | 6 | 2 | 31 | 3.07 |
| TAYLOR, RON | 491 | 799 | 45 | 43 | 391 | 353 | 464 | 209 | 17 | 3 | 0 | 72 | 3.93 |
| TERRELL, WALT | 125 | 816 | 49 | 45 | | | 404 | 342 | 123 | 21 | 8 | 0 | 3.89 |
| TERRY, RALPH | 338 | 1850 | 107 | 99 | | | 1000 | 446 | 257 | 75 | 20 | 11 | 3.62 |
| TIDROW, DICK | 620 | 1747 | 100 | 94 | | | 967 | 572 | 138 | 33 | 5 | 55 | 3.63 |
| TODD, JACKSON | 64 | 287 | 10 | 16 | | | 138 | 88 | 36 | 7 | 0 | 0 | 4.39 |
| TORREZ, MIKE | 494 | 3042 | 185 | 160 | | | 1404 | 1371 | 458 | 117 | 15 | 0 | 3.96 |
| TWITCHELL, WAYNE | 282 | 1064 | 46 | 65 | | | 789 | 537 | 133 | 15 | 6 | 2 | 3.94 |
| WAKEFIELD, BILL | 62 | 120 | 3 | 5 | | | 61 | 61 | 4 | 0 | 0 | 2 | 3.60 |
| WALTER, GENE | 72 | 120 | 2 | 4 | 53 | 47 | 102 | 57 | 0 | 0 | 0 | 4 | 3.53 |
| WEBB, HANK | 53 | 169 | 7 | 9 | | | 71 | 91 | 19 | 3 | 1 | 0 | 4.31 |
| WILLEY, CARL | 199 | 876 | 28 | 38 | | | 493 | 326 | 117 | 28 | 11 | 1 | 3.76 |
| WILLHITE, NICK | 58 | 182 | 6 | 12 | | | 118 | 75 | 29 | 3 | 1 | 1 | 4.55 |
| WILLIAMS, CHARLIE | 268 | 572 | 23 | 22 | | | 257 | 275 | 33 | 2 | 0 | 1 | 3.98 |
| ZACHRY, PAT | 283 | 1165. | 69 | 67 | | | 661 | 484 | 154 | 29 | 7 | 3 | 3.51 |

# Batting Record & Index

| PLAYER | G | AB | R | H | 2B | 3B | HR | RBI | SB | SLG | BB | SO | AVG |
|---|---|---|---|---|---|---|---|---|---|---|---|---|---|
| AGEE, TOMMIE | 1129 | 3912 | 558 | 999 | 170 | 27 | 130 | 433 | 167 | .412 | 342 | 918 | .255 |
| ALMON, BILL | 1148 | 3230 | 376 | 826 | 132 | 25 | 36 | 290 | 127 | .346 | 238 | 604 | .256 |
| ALOMAR, SANDY | 1481 | 4760 | 558 | 1168 | 126 | 19 | 13 | 282 | 227 | .288 | 302 | 482 | .245 |
| ALOU, JESUS | 1380 | 4345 | 448 | 1216 | 170 | 26 | 32 | 377 | 31 | .353 | 138 | 267 | .280 |
| ALTMAN, GEORGE | 991 | 3091 | 409 | 832 | 132 | 34 | 101 | 403 | 52 | .353 | 268 | 572 | .269 |
| ALVARADO, LUIS | 463 | 1160 | 116 | 248 | 43 | 4 | 5 | 84 | 11 | .271 | 47 | 160 | .214 |
| ASHBURN, RICHIE | 2189 | 8365 | 1322 | 2574 | 317 | 109 | 29 | 586 | 234 | .382 | 1198 | 571 | .308 |
| ASHFORD, TUCKER | 223 | 510 | 42 | 111 | 31 | 1 | 6 | 55 | 1 | .306 | 42 | 75 | .218 |
| ASPROMONTE, BOB | 1324 | 4369 | 386 | 1103 | 135 | 26 | 60 | 457 | 19 | .336 | 333 | 459 | .252 |
| AYALA, BENNY | 425 | 865 | 114 | 217 | 42 | 1 | 38 | 145 | 2 | .434 | 71 | 136 | .251 |
| BACKMAN, WALLY | 572 | 1775 | 272 | 506 | 77 | 13 | 6 | 125 | 86 | .353 | 194 | 243 | .285 |
| BAILOR, BOB | 955 | 2937 | 339 | 775 | 107 | 23 | 9 | 222 | 90 | .325 | 187 | 164 | .264 |
| BEANE, BILLY | 93 | 201 | 20 | 42 | 7 | 0 | 3 | 16 | 2 | .289 | 11 | 59 | .209 |
| BEAUCHAMP, JIM | 393 | 661 | 79 | 153 | 18 | 4 | 14 | 90 | 6 | .334 | 22 | 150 | .231 |
| BELL, GUS | 1741 | 6478 | 865 | 1823 | 311 | 66 | 206 | 942 | 30 | .445 | 470 | 636 | .281 |
| BERRA, YOGI | 2120 | 7555 | 1175 | 2150 | 321 | 49 | 358 | 1430 | 30 | .482 | 704 | 414 | .285 |
| BOCHY, BRUCE | 320 | 727 | 67 | 180 | 34 | 2 | 24 | 82 | 1 | .399 | 56 | 156 | .248 |
| BOISCLAIR, BRUCE | 410 | 917 | 114 | 241 | 47 | 6 | 10 | 77 | 18 | .360 | 86 | 183 | .263 |
| BOSCH, DON | 146 | 318 | 44 | 52 | 6 | 1 | 1 | 13 | 4 | .226 | 22 | 77 | .164 |
| BOSWELL, KEN | 930 | 2517 | 266 | 625 | 91 | 19 | 31 | 234 | 27 | .337 | 241 | 239 | .248 |
| BOUCHEE, ED | 670 | 2199 | 298 | 583 | 114 | 21 | 61 | 290 | 5 | .419 | 340 | 401 | .265 |
| BOWA, LARRY | 2161 | 8204 | 972 | 2141 | 255 | 95 | 15 | 510 | 313 | .321 | 461 | 547 | .261 |
| BOYER, KEN | 2034 | 7455 | 1104 | 2143 | 318 | 68 | 282 | 1141 | 105 | .462 | 713 | 1017 | .287 |
| BRADLEY, MARK | 90 | 113 | 13 | 23 | 5 | 0 | 3 | 5 | 4 | .354 | 11 | 36 | .204 |
| BRESSOUD, ED | 1186 | 3672 | 443 | 925 | 184 | 40 | 94 | 365 | 4 | .401 | 359 | 723 | .252 |
| BROOKS, HUBIE | 787 | 2964 | 313 | 822 | 137 | 23 | 55 | 377 | 38 | .396 | 187 | 464 | .278 |
| BUCHEK, JERRY | 421 | 1177 | 96 | 259 | 35 | 11 | 22 | 108 | 5 | .375 | 75 | 312 | .220 |
| BURRIGHT, LARRY | 159 | 356 | 44 | 73 | 8 | 6 | 4 | 33 | 5 | .295 | 29 | 92 | .205 |
| CANNIZZARO, CHRIS | 740 | 1950 | 132 | 458 | 66 | 12 | 18 | 169 | 3 | .309 | 241 | 354 | .235 |
| CARDENAL, JOSE | 2017 | 6964 | 936 | 1913 | 333 | 46 | 138 | 775 | 329 | .395 | 608 | 807 | .275 |
| CARMEL, DUKE | 124 | 227 | 22 | 48 | 7 | 3 | 9 | 23 | 3 | .322 | 27 | 60 | .211 |
| CARTER, GARY | 1689 | 6063 | 847 | 1646 | 287 | 26 | 271 | 999 | 36 | .461 | 680 | 763 | .271 |
| CHACON, ELIO | 228 | 616 | 89 | 143 | 15 | 5 | 4 | 39 | 20 | .292 | 111 | 109 | .232 |
| CHAPMAN, KELVIN | 172 | 421 | 51 | 94 | 17 | 2 | 3 | 34 | 13 | .295 | 33 | 60 | .223 |
| CHARLES, ED | 1005 | 3428 | 438 | 917 | 147 | 30 | 86 | 421 | 86 | .397 | 379 | 525 | .263 |
| CHILES, RICH | 284 | 618 | 68 | 157 | 37 | 8 | 6 | 76 | 1 | .350 | 50 | 65 | .254 |
| CHITI, HARRY | 502 | 1495 | 135 | 356 | 49 | 6 | 41 | 179 | 4 | .365 | 115 | 242 | .238 |
| CHRISTENSEN, JOHN | 56 | 124 | 12 | 24 | 6 | 1 | 3 | 16 | 2 | .331 | 20 | 25 | .194 |
| CHRISTOPHER, JOE | 638 | 1667 | 224 | 434 | 68 | 17 | 29 | 173 | 29 | .374 | 157 | 277 | .260 |
| CLENDENON, DONN | 1362 | 4648 | 594 | 1273 | 192 | 57 | 159 | 682 | 90 | .442 | 379 | 1140 | .274 |
| CLINES, GENE | 870 | 2328 | 314 | 645 | 85 | 24 | 5 | 187 | 71 | .341 | 169 | 271 | .277 |
| COLEMAN, CHOO | 201 | 462 | 51 | 91 | 8 | 2 | 9 | 30 | 7 | .281 | 37 | 85 | .197 |
| COLLINS, KEVIN | 201 | 388 | 30 | 81 | 17 | 4 | 6 | 34 | 1 | .320 | 20 | 97 | .209 |
| COOK, CLIFF | 163 | 398 | 33 | 80 | 17 | 3 | 7 | 35 | 2 | .312 | 26 | 136 | .201 |
| CORCORAN, TIM | 503 | 1043 | 119 | 283 | 46 | 4 | 12 | 128 | 7 | .358 | 128 | 102 | .271 |
| COWAN, BILLY | 493 | 1190 | 131 | 281 | 44 | 8 | 40 | 125 | 17 | .387 | 58 | 297 | .236 |
| CUBBAGE, MIKE | 703 | 1951 | 218 | 503 | 74 | 20 | 34 | 251 | 6 | .369 | 215 | 233 | .258 |
| DAVIS, TOMMY | 1999 | 7223 | 811 | 2121 | 272 | 35 | 153 | 1052 | 136 | .405 | 381 | 754 | .294 |
| DEMERIT, JOHN | 93 | 132 | 21 | 23 | 3 | 0 | 7 | 16 | 5 | .265 | 65 | 33 | .174 |
| DRAKE, SAMMY | 53 | 72 | 8 | 11 | 0 | 0 | 0 | 7 | 0 | .153 | 8 | 17 | .153 |
| DWYER, JIM | 1043 | 2128 | 304 | 543 | 95 | 16 | 56 | 268 | 20 | .394 | 299 | 295 | .255 |
| DYER, DUFFY | 722 | 1993 | 151 | 441 | 74 | 11 | 30 | 173 | 10 | .315 | 226 | 415 | .221 |
| DYKSTRA, LEN | 230 | 667 | 117 | 187 | 36 | 10 | 9 | 64 | 46 | .405 | 86 | 79 | .280 |
| ELLIOT, LARRY | 157 | 437 | 53 | 103 | 22 | 2 | 15 | 56 | 1 | .398 | 45 | 105 | .236 |

| PLAYER | G | AB | R | H | 2B | 3B | HR | RBI | SB | SLG | BB | SO | AVG |
|---|---|---|---|---|---|---|---|---|---|---|---|---|---|
| FERNANDEZ, CHICO | 856 | 2778 | 270 | 666 | 91 | 19 | 40 | 259 | 68 | .329 | 213 | 338 | .240 |
| FERRER, SERGIO | 125 | 178 | 41 | 43 | 3 | 4 | 0 | 3 | 7 | .303 | 17 | 27 | .242 |
| FITZGERALD, MIKE | 301 | 884 | 66 | 209 | 35 | 3 | 14 | 106 | 9 | .330 | 92 | 166 | .236 |
| FLORES, GIL | 185 | 464 | 58 | 121 | 20 | 6 | 2 | 37 | 15 | .343 | 34 | 61 | .261 |
| FLYNN, DOUG | 1308 | 3853 | 288 | 918 | 115 | 39 | 7 | 284 | 20 | .294 | 151 | 320 | .238 |
| FOLI, TIM | 1677 | 6010 | 575 | 1508 | 241 | 20 | 25 | 499 | 81 | .310 | 261 | 397 | .251 |
| FOSTER, GEORGE | 1890 | 6739 | 956 | 1861 | 301 | 44 | 334 | 1197 | 50 | .483 | 642 | 1358 | .276 |
| FOSTER, LEO | 144 | 262 | 35 | 52 | 8 | 0 | 2 | 26 | 7 | .252 | 22 | 44 | .198 |
| FOY, JOE | 716 | 2484 | 355 | 615 | 102 | 16 | 58 | 291 | 99 | .372 | 390 | 405 | .248 |
| FREGOSI, JIM | 1902 | 6523 | 844 | 1726 | 264 | 78 | 151 | 706 | 76 | .398 | 715 | 1097 | .265 |
| GALLAGHER, BOB | 213 | 265 | 34 | 56 | 6 | 2 | 7 | 13 | 16 | .275 | 16 | 56 | .220 |
| GARDENHIRE, RON | 285 | 710 | 57 | 165 | 27 | 3 | 4 | 49 | 13 | .296 | 46 | 122 | .232 |
| GARRETT, WAYNE | 1092 | 3285 | 438 | 786 | 107 | 22 | 61 | 340 | 38 | .341 | 561 | 529 | .239 |
| GASPAR, ROD | 178 | 260 | 35 | 54 | 7 | 0 | 1 | 17 | 8 | .250 | 33 | 29 | .208 |
| GILES, BRIAN | 199 | 545 | 53 | 127 | 20 | 2 | 5 | 37 | 23 | .407 | 48 | 109 | .233 |
| GONDER, JESSE | 395 | 876 | 73 | 220 | 28 | 2 | 26 | 94 | 1 | .377 | 72 | 184 | .251 |
| GOOSSEN, GREG | 193 | 460 | 33 | 111 | 24 | 1 | 13 | 44 | 1 | .383 | 42 | 112 | .241 |
| GOSGER, JIM | 705 | 1815 | 197 | 411 | 67 | 16 | 30 | 177 | 25 | .331 | 217 | 316 | .226 |
| GREEN, PUMPSIE | 344 | 796 | 119 | 196 | 31 | 12 | 13 | 74 | 12 | .364 | 138 | 132 | .246 |
| GRIEVE, TOM | 670 | 1907 | 200 | 474 | 76 | 10 | 65 | 254 | 7 | .401 | 135 | 424 | .249 |
| GROTE, JERRY | 1421 | 4339 | 352 | 1092 | 160 | 22 | 39 | 404 | 15 | .326 | 399 | 600 | .252 |
| GULDEN, BRAD | 165 | 413 | 43 | 85 | 14 | 4 | 5 | 42 | 2 | .286 | 43 | 56 | .206 |
| HAHN, DON | 454 | 997 | 104 | 235 | 38 | 4 | 7 | 74 | 11 | .303 | 122 | 158 | .236 |
| HAMPTON, IKE | 113 | 135 | 15 | 28 | 4 | 1 | 4 | 18 | 1 | .341 | 11 | 38 | .207 |
| HARKNESS, TIM | 259 | 562 | 59 | 132 | 18 | 4 | 14 | 61 | 7 | .356 | 58 | 118 | .235 |
| HARRELSON, BUD | 1533 | 4744 | 539 | 1120 | 136 | 45 | 7 | 267 | 127 | .288 | 633 | 653 | .236 |
| HEARN, ED | 49 | 136 | 16 | 36 | 5 | 0 | 4 | 10 | 0 | .390 | 12 | 19 | .265 |
| HEBNER, RICH | 1908 | 6144 | 865 | 1694 | 273 | 57 | 203 | 890 | 38 | .438 | 687 | 741 | .276 |
| HEEP, DANNY | 560 | 1313 | 144 | 338 | 71 | 5 | 20 | 149 | 9 | .376 | 153 | 175 | .257 |
| HEIDEMANN, JACK | 426 | 1093 | 94 | 231 | 27 | 4 | 9 | 75 | 3 | .268 | 78 | 203 | .211 |
| HEISE, BOBBY | 499 | 1144 | 104 | 283 | 43 | 3 | 3 | 86 | 5 | .293 | 47 | 77 | .247 |
| HENDERSON, KEN | 1444 | 4553 | 595 | 1168 | 216 | 26 | 122 | 576 | 86 | .396 | 589 | 763 | .257 |
| HENDERSON, STEVE | 986 | 3298 | 439 | 931 | 152 | 48 | 65 | 411 | 78 | .417 | 367 | 639 | .282 |
| HERNANDEZ, KEITH | 1721 | 6090 | 969 | 1840 | 372 | 59 | 128 | 900 | 96 | .445 | 917 | 795 | .302 |
| HICKMAN, JIM | 1421 | 3974 | 512 | 1002 | 163 | 25 | 159 | 560 | 17 | .426 | 491 | 832 | .252 |
| HICKS, JOE | 212 | 416 | 41 | 92 | 11 | 3 | 12 | 39 | 2 | .349 | 29 | 73 | .221 |
| HILLER, CHUCK | 704 | 2121 | 253 | 516 | 76 | 20 | 20 | 152 | 14 | .316 | 157 | 187 | .243 |
| HODGES, GIL | 2071 | 7030 | 1105 | 1921 | 295 | 48 | 370 | 1274 | 63 | .487 | 943 | 1137 | .273 |
| HODGES, RON | 666 | 1426 | 119 | 342 | 56 | 2 | 19 | 147 | 10 | .322 | 224 | 217 | .240 |
| HOWARD, FRANK | 1895 | 6488 | 864 | 1774 | 245 | 35 | 382 | 1119 | 8 | .499 | 782 | 1460 | .273 |
| HUNT, RON | 1483 | 5235 | 745 | 1429 | 223 | 23 | 39 | 370 | 65 | .403 | 555 | 882 | .273 |
| HURDLE, CLINT | 512 | 1388 | 161 | 359 | 81 | 12 | 32 | 193 | 7 | .259 | 176 | 260 | .259 |
| JOHNSON, DAVE A. | 874 | 2307 | 254 | 628 | 88 | 11 | 44 | 230 | 24 | .377 | 156 | 291 | .272 |
| JOHNSON, DAVE W. | 14435 | 4797 | 595 | 1252 | 242 | 18 | 136 | 609 | 33 | .404 | 559 | 675 | .261 |
| JOHNSON, HOWARD | 411 | 1185 | 145 | 299 | 51 | 5 | 40 | 154 | 31 | .405 | 128 | 249 | .252 |
| JONES, CLEON | 1213 | 4263 | 565 | 1196 | 183 | 33 | 93 | 524 | 91 | .404 | 360 | 702 | .281 |
| JORGENSEN, MIKE | 1633 | 3421 | 429 | 833 | 132 | 13 | 95 | 426 | 58 | .373 | 532 | 589 | .243 |
| KANEHL, ROD | 340 | 796 | 103 | 192 | 23 | 8 | 6 | 47 | 17 | .300 | 35 | 80 | .241 |
| KINGMAN, DAVE | 1941 | 6677 | 901 | 1575 | 240 | 25 | 442 | 1210 | 85 | .478 | 608 | 1816 | .236 |
| KLAUS, BOBBY | 215 | 590 | 65 | 123 | 25 | 4 | 5 | 29 | 5 | .295 | 74 | 92 | .208 |
| KLIMCHOCK, LOU | 318 | 669 | 64 | 155 | 21 | 3 | 13 | 69 | 3 | .330 | 31 | 71 | .232 |
| KNIGHT, RAY | 1240 | 3967 | 410 | 1102 | 230 | 25 | 67 | 497 | 13 | .399 | 284 | 459 | .278 |
| KOLB, GARY | 293 | 450 | 63 | 94 | 9 | 6 | 6 | 29 | 10 | .296 | 46 | 104 | .209 |
| KRANEPOOL, ED | 1853 | 5436 | 536 | 1418 | 225 | 25 | 118 | 614 | 15 | .377 | 454 | 581 | .261 |
| LANDRITH, HOBIE | 772 | 1929 | 179 | 450 | 69 | 12 | 34 | 203 | 5 | .327 | 253 | 188 | .233 |

## PLAYER

| PLAYER | G | AB | R | H | 2B | 3B | HR | RBI | SB | SLG | BB | SO | AVG |
|---|---|---|---|---|---|---|---|---|---|---|---|---|---|
| LEWIS, JOHNNY | 226 | 771 | 97 | 175 | 24 | 6 | 22 | 74 | 8 | .359 | 95 | 194 | .297 |
| LINZ, PHIL | 519 | 1372 | 185 | 322 | 64 | 4 | 11 | 96 | 13 | .311 | 112 | 195 | .235 |
| LUPLOW, AL | 481 | 1243 | 147 | 292 | 34 | 6 | 33 | 125 | 8 | .352 | 127 | 213 | .235 |
| MADDOX, ELLIOTT | 1029 | 2843 | 360 | 742 | 121 | 16 | 18 | 234 | 60 | .334 | 409 | 358 | .261 |
| MAGADAN, DAVE | 443 | 1530 | 271 | 495 | 90 | 11 | 4 | 234 | 6 | .405 | 345 | 174 | .324 |
| MANGUAL, PEPE | 319 | 972 | 155 | 235 | 35 | 6 | 16 | 83 | 64 | .340 | 147 | 238 | .242 |
| MANKOWSKI, PHIL | 269 | 739 | 72 | 195 | 23 | 4 | 8 | 64 | 3 | .338 | 55 | 103 | .264 |
| MANTILLA, FELIX | 969 | 2707 | 360 | 707 | 97 | 10 | 89 | 330 | 27 | .403 | 256 | 352 | .261 |
| MARSHALL, DAVE | 490 | 1049 | 123 | 258 | 41 | 4 | 16 | 114 | 13 | .333 | 133 | 239 | .246 |
| MARSHALL, JIM | 410 | 852 | 111 | 206 | 24 | 7 | 29 | 106 | 5 | .388 | 101 | 139 | .242 |
| MARTIN, J.C. | 908 | 2189 | 189 | 487 | 82 | 12 | 32 | 230 | 9 | .315 | 201 | 299 | .222 |
| MARTIN, JERRY | 1018 | 2652 | 337 | 666 | 130 | 17 | 85 | 345 | 38 | .409 | 207 | 574 | .251 |
| MARTINEZ, TED | 657 | 1480 | 165 | 355 | 50 | 16 | 7 | 108 | 29 | .309 | 55 | 213 | .240 |
| MAY, JERRY | 556 | 1527 | 120 | 357 | 63 | 10 | 15 | 130 | 1 | .318 | 157 | 293 | .234 |
| MAYS, WILLIE | 2992 | 10881 | 2062 | 3283 | 523 | 140 | 660 | 1903 | 338 | .557 | 1463 | 1526 | .302 |
| MAZZILLI, LEE | 1243 | 3758 | 514 | 987 | 176 | 23 | 84 | 406 | 183 | .389 | 555 | 562 | .263 |
| McMILLAN, ROY | 2093 | 6752 | 739 | 1639 | 253 | 35 | 68 | 594 | 41 | .321 | 665 | 711 | .243 |
| MERCADO, ORLANDO | 151 | 375 | 23 | 78 | 15 | 4 | 3 | 34 | 3 | .293 | 24 | 57 | .208 |
| MILLAN, FELIX | 1480 | 5791 | 699 | 1617 | 229 | 38 | 22 | 403 | 67 | .343 | 318 | 242 | .279 |
| MILNER, JOHN | 1215 | 3436 | 455 | 855 | 140 | 16 | 131 | 498 | 31 | .413 | 504 | 473 | .249 |
| MITCHELL, KEVIN | 115 | 342 | 51 | 94 | 22 | 2 | 12 | 44 | 3 | .456 | 33 | 64 | .275 |
| MONTANEZ, WILLIE | 1632 | 5843 | 645 | 1604 | 279 | 25 | 139 | 802 | 32 | .402 | 465 | 751 | .275 |
| MORALES, JERRY | 1441 | 4528 | 516 | 1173 | 199 | 36 | 95 | 570 | 37 | .382 | 366 | 567 | .259 |
| MORAN, AL | 135 | 353 | 28 | 69 | 9 | 2 | 1 | 27 | 3 | .229 | 38 | 62 | .195 |
| MURPHY, BILL | 84 | 135 | 15 | 31 | 4 | 1 | 3 | 13 | 1 | .341 | 7 | 34 | .230 |
| NAPOLEON, DANNY | 80 | 130 | 7 | 21 | 3 | 1 | 1 | 7 | 0 | .200 | 7 | 33 | .162 |
| NEAL, CHARLEY | 970 | 3316 | 461 | 858 | 113 | 38 | 87 | 391 | 48 | .394 | 337 | 557 | .259 |
| NOLAN, JOE | 621 | 1454 | 156 | 382 | 66 | 10 | 27 | 178 | 7 | .378 | 164 | 183 | .263 |
| NORMAN, DAN | 192 | 348 | 42 | 79 | 8 | 3 | 11 | 37 | 1 | .362 | 29 | 76 | .227 |
| OQUENDO, JOSE | 277 | 655 | 72 | 153 | 16 | 1 | 1 | 40 | 20 | .266 | 49 | 106 | .234 |
| ORTIZ, JUNIOR | 192 | 481 | 33 | 127 | 17 | 0 | 1 | 42 | 3 | .306 | 22 | 82 | .264 |
| OTIS, AMOS | 1998 | 7299 | 1092 | 2020 | 374 | 66 | 193 | 1007 | 341 | .425 | 757 | 1008 | .277 |
| PACIOREK, TOM | 1365 | 4061 | 488 | 1145 | 229 | 30 | 83 | 491 | 55 | .414 | 244 | 685 | .282 |
| PARKER, SALTY | 11 | 25 | 6 | 7 | 2 | 0 | 0 | 4 | 0 | .360 | 2 | 3 | .280 |
| PFEIL, BOBBY | 106 | 281 | 25 | 68 | 12 | 2 | 0 | 19 | 1 | .306 | 13 | 36 | .242 |
| PHILLIPS, MIKE | 712 | 1719 | 166 | 412 | 46 | 11 | 11 | 145 | 12 | .314 | 133 | 242 | .240 |
| PIERSALL, JIMMY | 1734 | 5890 | 811 | 1604 | 256 | 52 | 104 | 591 | 115 | .386 | 523 | 583 | .272 |
| PIGNATANO, JOE | 307 | 689 | 81 | 161 | 25 | 4 | 16 | 62 | 4 | .351 | 94 | 116 | .234 |
| RAJSICH, GARY | 98 | 205 | 23 | 55 | 11 | 3 | 3 | 17 | 1 | .395 | 22 | 42 | .268 |
| RAMIREZ, MARIO | 184 | 286 | 33 | 55 | 8 | 2 | 4 | 28 | 0 | .283 | 41 | 64 | .192 |
| RANDLE, LEN | 1138 | 3950 | 488 | 1016 | 145 | 40 | 27 | 322 | 156 | .335 | 372 | 505 | .257 |
| REYNOLDS, RONN | 97 | 239 | 16 | 49 | 7 | 1 | 3 | 13 | 0 | .272 | 14 | 61 | .205 |
| REYNOLDS, TOMMIE | 513 | 1170 | 141 | 265 | 35 | 5 | 12 | 87 | 12 | .296 | 117 | 166 | .226 |
| SAMUEL, AMADO | 144 | 368 | 23 | 79 | 18 | 0 | 3 | 25 | 1 | .288 | 16 | 82 | .215 |
| SANTANA, RAFAEL | 374 | 1089 | 94 | 267 | 41 | 2 | 3 | 71 | 1 | .295 | 76 | 116 | .245 |
| SCHAFFER, JIMMIE | 304 | 574 | 53 | 128 | 28 | 3 | 11 | 56 | 1 | .340 | 49 | 127 | .223 |
| SHAMSKY, ART | 665 | 1686 | 194 | 426 | 60 | 15 | 68 | 233 | 5 | .427 | 188 | 254 | .253 |
| SHELBY, JOHN | 491 | 1354 | 188 | 325 | 59 | 13 | 30 | 135 | 52 | .363 | 63 | 260 | .240 |
| SHERRY, NORM | 194 | 497 | 45 | 107 | 13 | 1 | 18 | 69 | 4 | .346 | 37 | 102 | .215 |
| SHIRLEY, BART | 75 | 162 | 15 | 33 | 4 | 1 | 1 | 11 | 0 | .241 | 14 | 28 | .204 |
| SINGLETON, KEN | 2082 | 7189 | 985 | 2029 | 317 | 25 | 246 | 1065 | 21 | .436 | 1263 | 1246 | .282 |
| SMITH, BOBBY GENE | 476 | 962 | 101 | 234 | 35 | 5 | 13 | 96 | 5 | .331 | 55 | 154 | .243 |
| SMITH, CHARLIE | 771 | 2484 | 228 | 594 | 83 | 18 | 69 | 281 | 7 | .370 | 130 | 565 | .239 |
| SMITH, DICK | 76 | 142 | 18 | 31 | 6 | 2 | 0 | 7 | 9 | .289 | 6 | 42 | .218 |
| SNIDER, DUKE | 2143 | 7161 | 1259 | 2116 | 358 | 85 | 407 | 1333 | 99 | .540 | 971 | 1237 | .295 |
| STAHL, LARRY | 730 | 1721 | 167 | 400 | 58 | 19 | 36 | 163 | 22 | .351 | 142 | 357 | .232 |
| STAIGER, ROY | 152 | 457 | 42 | 104 | 19 | 1 | 4 | 38 | 4 | .300 | 30 | 59 | .228 |
| STANTON, LEROY | 829 | 2575 | 294 | 628 | 114 | 13 | 77 | 358 | 36 | .388 | 236 | 636 | .244 |
| STAUB, RUSTY | 2951 | 9720 | 1189 | 2716 | 499 | 47 | 292 | 1466 | 47 | .431 | 1255 | 888 | .279 |
| STEARNS, JOHN | 810 | 2681 | 334 | 712 | 152 | 10 | 46 | 312 | 91 | .381 | 323 | 301 | .266 |

## PLAYER

| PLAYER | G | AB | R | H | 2B | 3B | HR | RBI | SB | SLG | BB | SO | AVG |
|---|---|---|---|---|---|---|---|---|---|---|---|---|---|
| STEPHENSON, JOHNNY | 451 | 989 | 83 | 214 | 37 | 3 | 12 | 93 | 0 | .296 | 63 | 118 | .216 |
| STRAWBERRY, DARRYL | 516 | 1810 | 292 | 471 | 84 | 20 | 108 | 343 | 100 | .508 | 267 | 496 | .260 |
| STUART, DICK | 1112 | 3997 | 506 | 1055 | 157 | 30 | 228 | 743 | 2 | .489 | 301 | 957 | .264 |
| SUDAKIS, BILL | 530 | 1548 | 177 | 362 | 56 | 7 | 59 | 214 | 9 | .393 | 169 | 313 | .234 |
| SULLIVAN, JOHN | 116 | 259 | 9 | 59 | 5 | 0 | 2 | 18 | 0 | .270 | 19 | 45 | .228 |
| SWEET, RICK | 272 | 736 | 62 | 172 | 23 | 1 | 6 | 57 | 6 | .292 | 60 | 73 | .234 |
| SWOBODA, RON | 927 | 2581 | 285 | 624 | 87 | 10 | 73 | 344 | 20 | .379 | 299 | 647 | .242 |
| TAVERAS, FRANK | 1150 | 4043 | 503 | 1029 | 144 | 44 | 2 | 214 | 300 | .313 | 249 | 474 | .255 |
| TAYLOR, BOB | 394 | 724 | 56 | 158 | 25 | 0 | 16 | 82 | 0 | .319 | 36 | 146 | .218 |
| TAYLOR, SAMMY | 473 | 1263 | 127 | 309 | 47 | 9 | 33 | 147 | 3 | .375 | 122 | 181 | .245 |
| TEUFEL, TIM | 409 | 1359 | 180 | 355 | 81 | 8 | 31 | 148 | 6 | .401 | 158 | 193 | .261 |
| THEODORE, GEORGE | 105 | 192 | 21 | 42 | 5 | 2 | 2 | 16 | 1 | .276 | 18 | 27 | .219 |
| THOMAS, FRANK | 1766 | 6235 | 792 | 1671 | 262 | 31 | 286 | 962 | 15 | .454 | 484 | 894 | .268 |
| THRONEBERRY, MARV | 480 | 1186 | 143 | 281 | 37 | 8 | 53 | 170 | 3 | .416 | 130 | 295 | .237 |
| TORRE, JOE | 2209 | 7874 | 996 | 2342 | 344 | 59 | 252 | 1185 | 23 | .452 | 779 | 1094 | .297 |
| TREVINO, ALEX | 672 | 1876 | 192 | 467 | 81 | 8 | 15 | 186 | 13 | .325 | 161 | 231 | .249 |
| UNSER, DEL | 1799 | 5215 | 617 | 1344 | 179 | 42 | 87 | 481 | 64 | .358 | 481 | 675 | .258 |
| VAIL, MIKE | 665 | 1604 | 146 | 447 | 71 | 11 | 34 | 219 | 3 | .400 | 80 | 310 | .279 |
| VALENTINE, BOBBY | 639 | 1698 | 176 | 441 | 59 | 9 | 12 | 157 | 27 | .326 | 140 | 134 | .260 |
| VALENTINE, ELLIS | 883 | 3128 | 375 | 873 | 168 | 15 | 121 | 470 | 59 | .458 | 178 | 454 | .279 |
| VERYZER, TOM | 996 | 2848 | 250 | 687 | 84 | 12 | 14 | 231 | 9 | .294 | 143 | 329 | .241 |
| WASHINGTON, CLAUDELL | 1529 | 5488 | 762 | 1524 | 275 | 61 | 130 | 665 | 270 | .421 | 386 | 1029 | .278 |
| WEIS, AL | 800 | 1578 | 195 | 346 | 45 | 11 | 7 | 115 | 55 | .275 | 117 | 299 | .219 |
| WESTRUM, WES | 919 | 2322 | 302 | 503 | 59 | 8 | 96 | 315 | 10 | .373 | 489 | 508 | .217 |
| WILSON, MOOKIE | 800 | 3015 | 451 | 834 | 124 | 49 | 40 | 249 | 238 | .390 | 168 | 497 | .277 |
| WINNINGHAM, HERM | 229 | 524 | 58 | 125 | 13 | 9 | 7 | 37 | 34 | .338 | 47 | 130 | .239 |
| WOODLING, GENE | 1796 | 5587 | 830 | 1585 | 257 | 63 | 147 | 830 | 29 | .431 | 920 | 477 | .284 |
| YOUNGBLOOD, JOEL | 1180 | 3327 | 419 | 890 | 168 | 23 | 74 | 382 | 58 | .399 | 304 | 538 | .268 |
| ZIMMER, DON | 1095 | 3283 | 353 | 773 | 130 | 22 | 91 | 352 | 45 | .372 | 246 | 678 | .235 |